THE

THRESHOLD COVENANT

OR

THE BEGINNING OF RELIGIOUS RITES

BY

H. CLAY TRUMBULL

Author of *"The Blood Covenant," "The Salt Covenant,"* etc.

The Threshold Covenant, H. Clay Trumbull
ISBN #0-89228-075-1

Copyright, © 2000,
   Impact Christian Books, Inc.
   332 Leffingwell Ave.,
   Kirkwood, MO 63122

Originally published in Edinburgh
T. & T. Clark, 1896

Cover Design: *Ideations*

Scripture quotations are from the Authorized King James
Version.

PUBLISHER'S PREFACE

As we approach the first Passover of a new millennium, we rejoice to be able to introduce to a new generation of Christians and scholars the great richness of foundational truths contained within the two complementary volumes by Dr. Trumbull, *The Threshold Covenant*, and *The Salt Covenant*.

At the time of their original publication slightly over a century ago, these two works were hailed throughout the world by that era's most eminent and renowned scholars in the fields of archeology, Egyptology and theology.

In our own era when many of the basic beliefs of orthodox Christianity have fallen prey to the encroachment of worldliness and laziness, it is both a great blessing and challenge to be confronted by the scholarship and excellent, yet simple presentation of the tremendous and revelatory truths contained within these volumes.

I believe your heart will thrill, as mine did, to discover what the Lord's "passing-over" really was... and, what the significance of salt was in covenanting. I believe that afterwards you, too, will find yourself discovering new truths and greater understanding in formerly confusing passages as you begin deciphering those mysterious passages using the keys of covenant-understanding.

Indeed, these truths are foundational, because it is impossible, as many pastors and writers have noted, for one to properly understand the Bible without understanding the fundamental truths of *covenants* and *covenanting*. The Old Testament is literally the Old "Covenant" and the New Testament is likewise, the New "Covenant," and both are based upon *blood* covenants. Thus, both Testaments, and therefore, all of Scripture presuppose a familiarity with, and an understanding of, *covenanting* (the methods and means of the making of a covenant) and, more to the point, of covenanting *in blood*.

Dr. Trumbull did a great service for the body of Christ with his initial volume *The Blood Covenant,* which is the only book cited by the Encyclopedia Britannica as a source for "covenants" or "covenanting in blood," and which we had the honor of reintroducing nearly twenty years ago. Thousands have since been blessed by our new edition of the book, and its republication has generated numerous additional volumes on the same subject. Perhaps these two books will also stimulate additional scholarship.

It is with a profound anticipation and excitement, that we present to the Body of Christ at the beginning of the new millennium the two companion volumes to *The Blood Covenant . . . The Salt Covenant* and *The Threshold Covenant.*

William D. Banks,
Publisher

Kirkwood, Missouri
Prior to Pentecost, 2000

iv

AUTHOR'S PREFACE

This work does not treat of the origin of man's religious faculty, or of the origin of the sentiment of religion; nor does it enter the domain of theological discussion. It simply attempts to show the beginning of religious rites, by which man evidenced a belief, however obtained, in the possibility of covenant relations between God and man; and the gradual development of those rites, with the progress of the race toward a higher degree of civilization and enlightenment. Necessarily the volume is not addressed to a popular audience, but to students in the lessons of primitive life and culture.

In a former volume, "The Blood Covenant," I sought to show the origin of sacrifice, and the significance of transferred or proffered blood or life. The facts given in that work have been widely accepted as lying at the basis of fundamental doctrines declared in the Hebrew and Christian Scriptures, and have also been recognized as the source of perverted views which have had prominence in the principal ethnic religions of the world. Scholars of as divergent schools of thought as Professors William Henry Green of Princeton, Charles A. Briggs of New York, George E. Day of Yale, John A. Broadus of Louisville, Samuel Ives Curtiss of Chicago, President Mark Hopkins of Williams, Rev. Drs. Alfred Edersheim of Oxford and Cunningham Geikie of Bournemouth, Professor Frederic Godet of Neuchatel, and many others, were agreed in recognizing the freshness and importance of its investigations, and the value of its conclusions. Professor W. Robertson Smith, of Cambridge, in thanking me for that work, expressed regret that he had not seen it before writing his "Kinship and Marriage in Early Arabia." He afterwards made repeated mention of the work as an authority in its field, in his Burnett Lectures on the "Religion of the Semites."

This volume grew out of that one. It looks back to a still earlier date. That began as it were with Cain and Abel, while this begins with Adam and Eve. It was while preparing a Supplement for a second edition of that volume that the main idea of this work assumed such importance in my mind that I was led to make a separate study of it, and present it independently. The special theory here advanced is wholly a result of induction. The special theory here advanced is wholly a result of induction. The theory came out of the gathered facts, instead of the facts being gathered in support of the theory.

Of course, these facts are not new, but it is believed that their synthetic arrangement is. It has been a favorite method with students of primitive religions to point out widely different objects of primitive worship and their corresponding cults among different peoples, and then to try to show how the ceremonials of the Hebrew and Christian Scriptures were made up from these primitive cults. But the course of investigation here pursued seems to show that the earlier cult was the simple one, which has been developed in the line of the Bible story, and that the other cults, even those baser and more degraded, are only natural perversions of the original simple one. This is a reversal of the usual order in studies of primitive religious rites. Here it is first the simple, then the complex; first the one germ, then the many varieties of growth from that germ.

As this particular subject of investigation seems to be a

hitherto untrodden field, I am unable to refer to any published works as my principal sources of information. But I have gathered important related facts from various directions, giving full credit in explicit footnotes, page by page. Many added facts confirmatory of my position might, undoubtedly, have been found through yet wider and more discerning research, and they will be brought to light by other gleaners in the same field. Indeed, a chief value of this volume will be in the fresh study it provokes on the part of those whom it stimulates to more thorough investigation in the direction here pointed out. And if such study shows an added agreement between some of the main facts of modern scientific investigation and those disclosed in the Bible narrative, that will not be a matter of regret to any fair-minded scholar.

In my earlier studies for this work, I had valuable assistance from the late Mr. John T. Napier; and in my later researches I have been materially assisted by Professors Herman V. Hilprecht, E. Washburn Hopkins, William R. Lamberton, John Henry Wright, Robert Ellis Thompson, Morris Jastrow, Jr., D. G. Brinton, Adolph Erman, Adolph Erman, W. Max Muller, W. Hayes Ward, M. B. Riddle, Minton Warren, Alfred Gudeman, John P. Peters, M. W. Easton, and A. L. Frothingham, Jr., President George Washburn, Rev. Drs. Marcus Jastrow, H. H. Jessup, George A. Ford, William W. Eddy, and Benjamin Labaree, Rev. William Ewing, Rev. Paulus Moort, Dr. Talcott Williams, Dr. J. Solis Cohen, Dr. A. T. Clay, Dr. T. H. Powers Sailer, Judge Mayer Sulzberger, Mr. S. Schecter, Mr. Frank Hamilton Cushing, Captain John G. Bourke, Mr. Khaleel Sarkis, Mr. John T. Haddad, Mr. Montague Cockle, Mr. Le Roy Bliss Peckham, the late Mr. William John Potts, and other specialists. To all these I return my sincere thanks.

Facts and suggestions that came to my notice after the main work was completed, or that, while known to me before, did not seem to have a place in the direct presentation of the argument, have been given a place in the Appendix. These may prove helpful to scholars who would pursue the investigation beyond my limits of treatment.

Comments of eminent specialists in Europe and America, to whom the proofsheets of the volume were submitted before publication, are given in a Supplement. Important additions are thus made to the results of my researches which are sure to be valued accordingly.

H. C. T.

Philadelphia,
Passover Week, 1896

CONTENTS

I.

PRIMITIVE FAMILY ALTAR

II.
EARLIEST TEMPLE ALTAR

III.
SACRED BOUNDARY LINE

IV.
ORIGIN OF THE RITE

V.
HEBREW PASS-OVER, OR CROSS-OVER, SACRIFICE

VI.
CHRISTIAN PASSOVER

VII.
OUTGROWTHS AND PERVERSIONS OF THIS RITE

APPENDIX

SUPPLEMENT

COMMENTS OF SPECIALISTS.

INDEX

THE

THRESHOLD COVENANT

OR

THE BEGINNING OF RELIGIOUS RITES

BY

H. CLAY TRUMBULL

I.

PRIMITIVE FAMILY ALTAR

1. A BLOOD WELCOME AT THE DOOR

The primitive altar of the family would seem to have been the threshold, or door-sill, or entrance-way, of the home dwelling-place. This is indicated by surviving customs, in the East and elsewhere among primitive peoples, and by the earliest historic records of the human race. It is obvious that houses preceded temples, and that the house-father was the earliest priest. Sacrifices for the family were, therefore, within or at the entrance of the family domicile.

In Syria and in Egypt, at the present time, when a guest who is worthy of special honor is to be welcomed to a home, the blood of a slaughtered, or a "sacrificed," animal is shed on the threshold of that home, as a means of adopting the newcomer into the family, or of making a covenant union with him. And every such primitive covenant in blood includes an appeal to the protecting Deity to ratify it as between the two parties and himself.[1] While

---

[1] See Trumbull's *Blood Covenant*, passim.

3

the guest is still outside, the host takes a lamb, or a goat, and, tying its feet together, lays it upon the threshold of his door. Resting his left knee upon the bound victim, the host holds its head by his left hand, while with his right he cuts its throat. He retains his position until all the blood has flowed from the body upon the threshold. Then the victim is removed, and the guest steps over the blood, across the threshold; and in this act he becomes, as it were, a member of the family by the Threshold Covenant.

The flesh of the slaughtered animal is usually given to the neighbors, although in the case of humbler persons it is sometimes used for the meal of the guest in whose honor it is sacrificed. It may be a larger offering than a lamb or a goat, or it may be a smaller one. Sometimes several sheep are included in the sacrifice. Again, the offering may be a bullock or a heifer, or simply a fowl or a pair of pigeons. The more costly the gift, in proportion to the means of the host, the greater the honor to him who is welcomed.

As illustrative of this idea, a story is commonly told in Syria of a large-hearted man who gave proof of his exceptional devotedness to an honored guest. He had a horse which he prized as only an Oriental can prize and love one. This horse he sent to meet his guest, in order that it might bring him to the home of its owner. When the guest reached the house and dismounted, he spoke warm words in praise of the noble animal. At once the host led the horse to the house door, and cut its throat over the threshold, asking the guest to step over the blood of this costly offering, in acceptance of the proffered Threshold Covenant.

"If you know that one is coming whom you would honor and welcome, you must make ready to have the blood on the threshold when he appears," said a native Syrian. In case an honored guest arrives unexpectedly, so that there is no time to prepare the customary sacrifice, salt, as representing blood, may be sprinkled on the threshold, for the guest to pass over; or again coffee, as the Muhammadan substitute for the "blood of the grape,"[1] may be poured on it.[2]

Crossing the threshold, or entering the door, of a house, is in itself an implied covenant with those who are within, as shown by the earlier laws of India. He who goes in by the door must count himself, and must be recognized, as a guest, subject to the strictest laws of hospitality. But if he enters the house in some other way, not crossing the threshold, there is no such implied covenant on his part. He may then even despoil or kill the head of the house he has entered, without any breach of the law of hospitality, or the moral law as there understood.[3] Illustrations of this truth are found in the Mahabharata, as applicable to both a house and a city.[4] "It is in accordance with the strict law of all the law books," of ancient India, "that one may enter his foe's house by *a-dvāra*, 'not by door,' but his friend's house only 'by

---

1. See Trumbull's *Blood Covenant*, pp. 191 f., 370; also Frazer's *Golden Bough*, I., 183-185.

2. These facts I have obtained at different times in personal conversations with intelligent natives of Syria and of Egypt. It will be seen, later, how they are verified in the record of similar customs elsewhere.

3. See Hopkins's *Religions of India*, p. 362f.

4. *Ibid.*, with references to Mahabharata, 11., 21, 14, 53; X., 8, 10.

door."[1]

It would seem to have been in accordance with this primitive law of the East that Jesus said: "He that entereth not by the door into the fold of the sheep, but climbeth up some other way, the same is a thief and a robber. But he that entereth in by the door is the shepherd of the sheep . . . I am the door; by me if any man enter in, he shall be saved, and shall go in and go out, and shall find pasture. The thief cometh not, but that he may steal, and kill, and destroy: I came that they may have life, and may have it abundantly."[2]

It is possible that there is an explanation, in this law of the doorway, or threshold, of the common practice among primitive Scandinavians of attacking the inmates of an enemy's house through the roof instead of by the door;[3] also, of the custom in Greece of welcoming a victor in the Olympian games into his city through a breach in the walls, instead of causing him to enter by the gates, with its implied subjection to all the laws of hospitality.[4] (See Appendix.)

Examples of the blood welcome at the threshold abound in modern Egyptian customs. When the new khedive came to his palace, in 1882, a threshold sacrifice was offered as his welcome. "At the entrance to the palace

---

[1] *Ibid.*, with references to Laws of Manu, IV.,73, and to Gaut. 9:32.

[2] John 10:1, 2, 9, 10.

[3] See Lund's *Everyday Life in Scandinavia in the Sixteenth Century*, p.16, with note 36; also, the *Njals Saga*.

[4] See Smith's *Dict. of Greek and Roman Antiq.*, s. vv. "Athletae" and "Olympic Games"; also Gardner's *New Chapters in Greek History*, p. 299.

six buffaloes were slaughtered, two being killed just as the khedive's carriage reached the gateway. The blood of the animals was splashed across the entrance, so that the horses' hoofs and wheels of the carriage passed through it. The flesh was afterwards distributed among the poor."[1]

When General Grant was at Assioot, on the Upper Nile, during his journey around the world, he was doubly welcomed as a guest by the American vice-counsul, who was a native of Egypt. A bullock was sacrificed at the steamer landing, and its head was laid on one side of the gangplank, and its body on the other. The outpoured blood was between the head and the body, under the gangland, so that, in stepping from the steamer to the shore, General Grant would cross over it. When he reached the house of the vice-consul, a sheep was similarly sacrificed at the threshold, in such a way that General Grant passed over the blood in entering.

It is also said in Egypt: "If you buy a dahabiyeh," and therefore are to cross its threshold for the occupancy of your new home on the water, "you must, kill a sheep, letting the blood flow on the deck, or side, of the boat, in order that it may be lucky. Your friends will afterwards have to dine on the sheep."[2] There seems, indeed, to be a survival of this idea in the custom of "christening" a ship at the time of its launching, in England and America, a bottle of wine--the "blood of the grape"[3] —being broken on the bow of the

---

[1] See *London Folk-Lore Journal*, 1., 92.

[2] Prof. A. H. Sayce, in *London Folk-Lore*, 1., 523.

[3] Comp. with p.5, supra.

vessel as it crosses the threshold of the deep. And a feast usually follows this ceremony also.[1]

In Zindero, or Gingiro, or Zinder, in Central Africa, a new king is welcomed at the royal residence with a bloody threshold offering. "Before he enters his palace two men are to be slain; one at the foot of the tree by which his house is chiefly supported; the other at the threshold of his door, which is besmeared with the blood of the victim. And it is said . . . that the particular family, whose privilege it is to be slaughtered, so far from avoiding it, glory in the occasion, and offer themselves willingly to meet it."[2]

Among the Arabs in Central Africa, the blood welcome of a guest at the threshold of a home is a prevailing custom. "The usual welcome upon the arrival of a traveler, who is well received in an Arab camp, is the sacrifice of a fat sheep, that should be slaughtered at the door of the hut or tent, so that the blood flows to the threshold."[3]

On the arrival of strangers among the primitive tribes of Liberia, in West Africa, a fowl is killed, and its blood is sprinkled at the doorway.[4]

Receiving an honored guest with bread and salt, at the threshold of the house he enters, is common in Russia. Bread and salt are symbolic, in primitive thought, of flesh and blood. This threshold welcome seems to be a survival

---

[1] Comp. with p.71 f., infra.

[2] Bruce's *Travels*, Bk. II., p.514

[3] Baker's *Nile Tributaries of Abyssinia*, p.137; comp. 126 f.

[4] On the testimony of a Liberian colored clergyman.

of the threshold sacrifice.[1]

To step over or across the blood, or its substitute, on the door-sill, is to accept or ratify the proffered covenant; but to trample upon the symbol of the covenant is to show contempt for the host who proffers it, and no greater indignity than this is known in the realm of primitive social intercourse.

2. REVERENCE FOR THE THRESHOLD ALTAR.

The threshold, as the family altar on which the sacrificial blood of a covenant, welcome is poured out, is counted sacred, and is not to be stepped upon, or passed over lightly; but it is to be crossed over reverently, as in recognition of Him to whom all life belongs. "On passing the threshold," in Arabia, "it is proper to say, 'Bismillah,' that is, 'In the name of God.' Not to do so would be looked upon as a bad augury, alike for him who enters and for those within."[2] In Syria the belief prevails "that it is unlucky to tread on a threshold." When they receive a new member to their sect, the Bektashi derwishes of Syria bring him to the threshold, and prayers and sacrifices are offered "on the door-sill."[3]

"The khaleffs of Bagdad required all those who entered their palace to prostrate themselves on the threshold of the

[1] See, for example, Sir Robert Ker Porter's *Travels*, p.36f.

[2] Palgrave's *Personal Narrative of a Journey Through Central and Eastern Arabia*, I., 51.

[3] Conder's *Heth and Moab*, pp. 290, 293.

gate, where they had inserted a fragment of the black stone of the temple at Meccah, in order to render it (the threshold) more venerable to those who had been accustomed to press their foreheads against it. The threshold was of some height, and it was a crime to set foot upon it." In the advice which Nurshivan gives to his son Hormuz, he recommends him to betake himself to the threshold of the Lord; that is, to the "presence of God, in the same fashion in which the poor do, at the gates of the rich. 'Since you are his slave,' he says, 'set your forehead on his threshold.'"[1]

Among the Hindoos, "the threshold is . . . sacred in private houses; it is not propitious for a person to remain on it; neither to eat, sneeze, yawn, nor spit whilst there."[2]

A double welcome is sometimes given to one who is in an official position. Thus, a Syrian, who held a commission from the chief officer of customs in Upper Syria, was surprised at having two sheep sacrificed before him as he approached the door of a house east of the Sea of Galilee; and he graciously protested against the excessive honor shown him. "One sheep is to welcome yourself as a man, and the other is to welcome you as an officer of the government," was the answer. Loyalty as well as hospitality was indicated in these threshold sacrifices.

Sacredness attaches to the threshold in Persia. It must not be trodden on; but it is often kissed by those who would step over it.[3]

---

[1] D'Herbelot's *Bibliotheque Orientale*, s.v."Bab," p. 157.

[2] Robert's *Oriental Illus. Of Scrip.*, p. 149.

[3] Morier's *Second Journey Through Persia*, p. 254.

A man should always cross himself when he steps over a threshold in Russia; and, in some portions of the realm, it is believed that he ought not to sit down on the threshold. [1]

High sills, or thresholds, so that one must step over, and not on, them, are in the houses of Finland, and in the houses of many Finns in the United States. [2] The same was true of many Teutonic houses. [3]

To shake hands across a threshold, instead of crossing it, is said, in Finland, to ensure a quarrel. [4] To step over a threshold is, in Lapland, to bring one under the protection of the family within, and of its guardian deity. [5] The same is true among the Magyars. [6]

The ancient Pythagoreans quoted various maxims, supposed to be from the sayings of their great founder, as teaching important lessons for all time. In these maxims there were indications of a peculiar reverence for the threshold and doorway. Thus: "He who strikes his foot against the threshold should go back"; it were unsafe to pursue a movement so inauspiciously begun. And, again: "The doors should be kissed fondly by those who enter or

---

[1] Ralston's *Songs of the Russian People*, p. 137.

[2] On the testimony of a Finnish American.

[3] Lund's *Every-day Life in Scandinavia in the Sixteenth Century*, p. 12f.

[4] Jones and Kropf's *Folk-tales of Magyars,* p. 410, note.

[5] *Ibid.*, p. 410f.

[6] *Ibid.*, p. 259.

depart."[1]

"Treading on the threshold was . . . tabooed by the Tatars."[2] Again, on the other side of the globe, in Samoa, to spill water on the door-step, or threshold, when food is brought in, is a cause of anger to the protecting deity of the family. It may drive him away.[3]

In Europe and in America it is by many counted an ill omen to tread upon the threshold of the door on entering a house. To the present day, in portions of Scotland, the idea popularly prevails, that to tread directly upon the boundary lines of division between ordinary flagstones is to endanger one's soul; hence the very children are careful to avoid stepping upon those lines, in their walking across the courtyards or along the streets, in their everyday passing.

Many a person in the United States, who knows nothing of any superstition connected with this, avoids, if possible, stepping on, instead of over, the cracks or seams of a board walk, or even the seams of a carpet.

All these customs seem to be a survival of the feeling that the threshold is sacred as the primitive altar.

Apart from the reverence for the threshold demanded of those who pass over it, there is an obvious sanctity of the threshold recognized in the placing of images and amulets underneath it, and in the sacrifices and offerings placed on

---

[1] *Fragmenta Philosophorum Gracorum* (ed. Mullach), I., 510.

[2] See *Marriage Customs of the Mordvins*," in *London Folk-Lore*, I., 459, note; also Bergeron's *Voyage De Calpin*," cap. 10, cited in Burder's *Oriental Customs* (2d ed.), p. 24.

[3] Turner's *Samoa*, p. 37.

it, as a means of guarding the dwelling within.

In the building of private houses, as well as temples, and city gateways, in ancient Assyria, images of various kinds and sizes, "in bronze, red jasper, yellow stone, and baked earth . . . are buried beneath the stones of the threshold, so as to bar the entrance to all destructive spirits." Invocations are graven upon these figures.[1]

Herodotus mentions[2] that, in the annual feast in honor of the god Osiris, "every Egyptian sacrifices a hog before the door of his house" on the evening before the festival. Osiris was the God who was the judge of the soul after death, and who in a peculiar sense stood for the truth of the life to come. Every Egyptian desired, above all, to be in loving covenant with Osiris, and when he would offer a welcoming sacrifice to him, he did so before the door of his own house, as before the primitive family altar. That it was the *blood* poured out at the threshold which was the essential act of covenanting in this sacrifice to Osiris, is evidenced in the fact that the animal sacrificed was not eaten in the family of the sacrificer, but was carried away by the swineherd who furnished it.

Bunches of grass dipped in blood, and touched by the king, as if made representative of his dignity and power, are today placed on the threshold, as an offering, and as averters of evil in Equatorial Africa. This is known there as an ancient custom. In Uganda, "every house has charms hung

---

[1] See Maspero's *Life in Ancient Egypt and Assyria*, pp. 195,219.

[2] Rawlinson's *History of Herodotus*, II., 47,48.

on the door, and others laid on the threshold." An offering to the *lubare*, or local spirit, must be thrown across the threshold, from within the house, before a native ventures to leave his home in the morning.[1] Charms for this purpose are kept behind the door.

One of the requirements in the Vedic law (the sacred law of the Hindoos) was, that "on the door-sill (a bali must be placed) with a mantra addressed to Antariksha (the air),"[2] by a house father, in his home; that is, that an offering with an invocation to a deity, should be a sacrifice at the threshold altar. Other references in the Hindoo laws seem to demand bali offerings "at all the doors, as many as they are," in a house and evidence the importance and sacredness attaching to the doorway.[4]

The threshold seems to have special reverence in Northwestern India, in connection with the seasons of seedtime and harvest. At seedtime "a cake of cowdung formed into a cup" is placed on the threshold of the householder; it is filled with corn, and then water is poured over it as a libation to the deities. Cowdung is not only a

----

[1] Mackay's *Mackay of Uganda*, pp. 112f., 177.

[2] See "Sacred Laws of the Aryas." II., 2,4, in *Sacred Books of the East*, II., 107.

[3] "A *bali* is an offering of any sort, such as a handful of rice, flung to birds or spirits or waters, or to any supernatural beings. A *mantra* is a Vedic text, a verse muttered during a religious cere mony; often used in incantations, or in legitimate services to a god." - Prof. Dr. E. W. Hopkins.

[4] See "Sacred Laws of the Aryas." II., 12, in *Sacred Books of the East*, II., 200, 233.

14

means of enrichment to the soul, but it is a gift from the sacred cow, and so, in a sense, represents or stands for the life of the cow. It is laid on the threshold altar as an offering of life. The libation of water is an accompaniment of that offering; water is essential to life and growth, and it is a gift of the gods accordingly. Seed-sowing is recognized as an act which needs the blessing of the gods, and on which that blessing is sought in covenant relations.

At early harvest time the first-fruits of the grain-field are not taken to the threshing floor, but are brought home to be presented to the gods at the household altar, and afterwards eaten by the family, with a portion given to the Brahmans. The first bundle of corn is deposited at the threshold of the home, and a libation of water is made as a completion of its offering. The grain being taken from the ear, of a portion of this first-fruits, is mixed with milk and sugar, and every member of the family tastes it seven times.[1]

Among the Prabhus of Bombay, at the time of the birth of a child, an iron crowbar is placed "along the threshold of the room of confinement, as a check against the crossing of any evil spirit." This is in accordance with a Hindoo belief that evil spirits keep aloof from iron, "and even nowadays pieces of horseshoe can be seen nailed to the bottom sills of doors of native houses."[2] Iron seems, in various lands, to be deemed of peculiar value as a guard against evil spirits, and the threshold to be the place for its efficacious fixing.

---

[1] See Sir Henry M. Elliot's *Races of the Northwestern Provinces of India* (Beames's ed.), I., 197.

[2] See report of a meeting of the Bombay Anthropological Society, in *London Folk-Lore Journal*, VI., p.77.

Similarly, "in East Bothnia, when the cows are taken out of their winter quarters for the first time, an iron bar is laid before the threshold, over which all the cows must pass; for, if they do not, there will be nothing but trouble with them all the following summer."[1]

Among the folk customs in the line of exorcism and divination in Italy, the threshold has prominence. "In Tuscany, much taking of magical medicine is done on the threshold; it also plays a part in other sorcery."[2] A writer mentions a method of exorcism with incense, where three pinches of the best incense, and three of the second quality, are put in a row on the threshold of the door, and then, after other incense is burned within the house in an earthen fire-dish, these "little piles of incense on the threshold of the door" are lighted, with words of invocation. This process is repeated three times over.[3]

A method of curing a disorder of the wrist prevalent in harvest time, in North Germany, is by taking "three pieces of three-jointed straw," and so laying them "side by side as to correspond joint by joint," then chopping through the first joint into the block beneath. This "ceremony is performed on the threshold, and ends with the sign of the cross."[4]

Observances with reference to the threshold are numerous in Russia. "On it a cross is drawn to keep off

[1] Jones and Kropf's *Folk-Tales of Magyars*, p. 410 f., note.

[2] Leland's *Etruscan Roman Remains in Popular Tradition*, p. 282.

[3] *Ibid.*, p. 321 f.

[4] Jones and Kropf's *Folk-Tales of Magyars,* p. 332f.

maras (hags). Under it the peasants bury stillborn children. In Lithuania, when a new house is being built, a wooden cross, or some article which has been handed down from past generations, is placed under the threshold. There also when a newly baptized child is being brought back from church, it is customary for its father to hold it for a while over the threshold, 'so as to place the new member of the family under the protection of the domestic divinities' [bringing it newly into the family covenant at the threshold altar] . . . Sick children, who are supposed to have been afflicted by an evil eye, are washed on the threshold of their cottage, in order that, with the help of the Penates who reside there, the malady may be driven out of doors."[1]

At the annual feast known as "Death Week," among Slavonic peoples, marking the close of winter and the beginning of spring, the peasants in rural Russia combine for a sacrifice to appease the "Vodyaoui," or aroused water-spirit of the thawing streams. They also prepare a sacrifice for the "Domovoi" or house-spirit. A fat black pig is killed, and cut into as many pieces as there are residents in the place. "Each resident receives one piece, which he straightway buries under the doorstep at the entrance to his house. In some parts, it is said, the country folk bury a few eggs beneath the threshold of the dwelling to propitiate the 'Domovoi.'"[2]

When a Magyar maiden would win the love of a young

---

[1] Ralston's *Songs of the Russian People,* p. 136 f.

[2] See "Death Week in Russia," in *the Spectator* (London), for June 18, 1892.

man, or would bring evil on him because of his reluctance, she seeks influence over him by means of the sacred threshold. "She must steal something from the young man, and take it to a witch, who adds to it three beans, three bulbs of garlic, a few pieces of dry coal, and a dead frog. These are all put into an earthenware pot, and placed under the threshold," with a prayer for the object of her desire.[1]

A superstition is prevalent in Roumania, that if a bat, together with a gold coin, be buried under the threshold, there is "good luck" to the house.[2] Various superstitions, in connection with the bat are found among primitive peoples.[3]

In Japan, the threshold of the door is sprinkled with salt, after a funeral, and as a propitiatory sacrifice in time of danger.[4] Salt represents blood.

Among the Dyaks of Borneo, a pig's blood is sprinkled at the doorway to atone for the sin of unchastity by a daughter of the family. Again, the blood of a fowl is sprinkled there at the annual festival of seed-sowing, with prayers for fecundity and fertility.[5]

"On New Year's morning along the coast (in Aberdeenshire) where seaweed is gathered, a small quantity is

---

[1] Jones and Kropf's *Folk-Tales of Magyars*, p. 332

[2] On the testimony of a native Roumanian.

[3] See, for example, Turner's *Samoa*, pp. 21, 56 f., 216, 241; also Strack's *Der Blutaberglaube* (4th ed.), p. 39.

[4] Griffis's *Mikado's Empire*, pp. 467, 470; also, Isabella Bird's *Untrodden Tracks in Japan*, I., 392.

[5] St. John's *Life in the Far East*, I., 64, 157f.

laid down at each door of the farm-steading [the buildings of the homestead], as a means of bringing good luck." And fire and salt are put on the threshold of the byre-door before a cow leaves the building after giving birth to a calf.[1]

Of portions of Ireland, it was said, early in this century: "On the 11th of November, every family of a village kills an animal of some kind or other; those who are rich kill a cow or sheep, others a goose or a turkey; while those who are poor . . . kill a hen or a cock, and sprinkle the threshold with the blood, and do the same in the four corners of the house . . . to exclude every kind of evil spirit from the dwelling."[2]

Holes bored in the door-sill, and plugged with pieces of paper on which are written incantations, a broom laid across the door-sill, or "three horseshoes nailed on the door-step with toes up," are supposed to be a guard against witches or evil spirits in portions of Pennsylvania today.[3] Many a Pennsylvanian is unwilling to cross, for the first time, the threshold of a new home, without carrying salt and a Bible.

Among the Indians in ancient Mexico there was an altar near the door of every house, with instruments of sacrifice, and accompanying idols.[4]

"Threshold" and "foundation" are terms that are used interchangeably in primitive life. The sacredness of the

---

[1] See *London Folk-Lore Journal*, II., 330 f.

[2] Dr. Strean in *Mason's Statistical Account*, or *Parochial Survey of Ireland*, II., 75.

[3] See J. G. Owens on "Folk-Lore from Buffalo Valley, Central Pennsylvania," in *Journal of American Folk-lore*, IV., 126.

[4] B. Biaz's "Memoirs:" cited in Spencer's *Descriptive Sociology*, II., 23.

threshold-stone of a building pivots on its position as a foundation stone, a beginning stone, a boundary stone. Hence the foundation stone of any house, or other structure was sacred as the threshold of that building. According to Dr. H. V. Hilprecht, in the earlier buildings of Babylonia the inscriptions and invocations and deposits were at the threshold, and later under the four corners of the building; but when they were at the threshold they were not under the corners, and *vice versa*. It would seem from this that the cornerstone was recognized as the beginning, or the limit, or the threshold, of the building. It may be, therefore, that the modern ceremonies at the laying of a "cornerstone" are a survival of the primitive sacredness of a threshold-laying.[1]

It would seem, moreover, as if the sanctity of the threshold as the primitive altar were, in many places, in the course of time transferred to the family hearth. In the primitive tent the household fire was at the entrance way, as it is in the tents of the East today. Where Arabs have camped on an Eastern desert, the place of the shaykh's tent can always be known by the blackened hearthstones at its entrance, or threshold, where he welcomed guests to the hospitality of his tribe and family by the sharing of bread and salt, or by the outpouring of the blood of a slaughtered lamb or kid.

If, indeed, the earliest dwelling of man was a cave, rather than a tent, the household fire was still at its entrance, and the threshold was the hearthstone. When, in the progress of building-changes, the hearthstone was removed to the center of the building, or of the inner court, its

---

[1] See pp. 51, 55, infra.

sanctity went with it, as the place of the family fire. Thus, for example, in Russia, the Domovoi, or household deity, who is honored and invoked at the threshold, "is supposed to live behind the stove now, but in early times he, or the spirits of the dead ancestors, of whom he is now the chief representative, were held to be in even more direct relations with the fire on the hearth; as were the Penates of the Romans, who were sometimes spoken of as at the threshold, and again as at the hearth."[1]

A recognition of the peculiar sacredness of the threshold is shown, in different hands, by the popular unwillingness to have the dead carried over it on the way to burial. In India, the body of one dying in certain phases of the moon can in no wise be carried over the threshold. The house wall must be broken for its removal.[2] When Chinese students are attending the competitive examinations for promotion, they are shut up in rooms until their work is completed. If one of them dies at such a time, "the body is removed over the back wall, as the taking out openly through the front door would be regarded as an evil omen."[3]

In the capital of Korea there is a small gate in the city wall known as the "Gate of the Dead," through which alone a dead body can be carried out. But no one can ever enter through that passageway.[4]

---

[1] See Ralston's i, p.120.

[2] See Du Bois' *Description of the Character, Manners, and Customs of the Peoples of India*, II., 27. Compare pp. 5-7. supra.

[3] Nevius' *China and the Chinese*, p. 60.

[4] Landor's *Corea* or *Cho-sen*, p. 118.

There is a recognition, in Russian folk-tales, of safety to the spirit of one who dies in a house, if his body be passed out *under* the threshold of the outer door.[1]

It is not allowable to carry out a corpse through the main door of a house in Italy. There is a smaller door, in the side wall, known as the *porta di morti,* which is kept closed except as it is opened for the removal of a body at the time of a funeral.[2]

In Alaska, it is deemed an evil omen for the dead to be carried over the threshold. "Therefore the dying one, instead of being allowed to rest in peace in his last hours, is hastily lifted from his couch and put out of doors [or out of the house] by a hole in the rear wall" so as not to have a corpse pass the threshold.[3]

In some communities, in both Europe and America, the coffin is passed out of the house through the window, instead of through the door, at a funeral. And again, the front door is closed and a window is opened at the time of a death, in order that the spirit may pass out of the house in some other way than over the threshold.[4]

Even though the dead may not be lifted over the threshold altar, the dead may be buried underneath it. In both the far East and the far West, burials under the threshold are known. And in Christian churches of Europe,

---

[1] See Ralston's *Russian Folk-Tales,* p. 28 f.

[2] On the testimony of Professor Dr. A. L. Frothingham, Jr.

[3] Julia McNair Wright's *Among the Alaskans,* p. 313.

[4] Comp. Plutarch's *Roman Questions,* Q.5.

a grave underneath the altar is an honored grave for saint or ecclesiastic.

In the Apocalypse the seer beheld "underneath the altar the souls of them that had been slain for the word of God, and for the testimony which they held: and they cried with a great voice, saying, How long, O Master, the holy and true, dost thou not judge and avenge our blood on them that dwell on the earth?"[1]

3. THRESHOLD COVENANTING IN THE MARRIAGE CEREMONY

Marriage customs in various parts of the world, in ancient and modern times, illustrate this idea of the sacredness of the threshold as the family altar.

In portions of Syria, when a bride is brought to her husband's home, a lamb or a kid is sacrificed on the threshold, and she must step across the outpoured blood.[2] This marks her adoption into that family.

Among the wide-spreading 'Anazeh Bed'ween, the most prominent and extensive tribe of desert Arabs, whose range is from the Sinaitic Peninsula to the upper Desert of Syria, "when the marriage day is fixed, the bridegroom comes with a lamb in his arms to the tent of the father of his bride, and then, before witnesses, he cuts its throat. As soon as the blood falls upon the earth [and the earth is the only

---

[1] Rev. 6:9-10.

[2] On the testimony of an eye-witness.

threshold of a tent], the marriage ceremony is regarded as complete."[1] "In Egypt, the Copts sacrifice a sheep as the bride steps into the bridegroom's house, and she is compelled to step over the blood which flows upon the threshold in the doorway."[2] It is evident, moreover, that this custom is not confined to the Copts.[3]

Blood on the threshold, as an accompaniment of a marriage, is still counted important among Armenian Christians in Turkey. After the formal marriage ceremony at the church, the wedded pair, with their friends, proceed to the bridegroom's home. "At the moment of their arrival a sheep is sacrificed on the threshold, over the blood of which the wedding party steps to enter the house."[4]

In the island of Cyprus, a bridegroom is borne to the house of his bride on the wedding morning, in a living chair formed by the crossed hands of his neighbor friends. Dismounting at her door, "as he is about to pass in, a fowl is brought and held down by head and feet upon the threshold of the door; the bridegroom takes an axe, cuts off the head, and only then may he enter."[5]

Like customs are found among yet more primitive peoples. Thus, for instance, with the western Somali tribes, in

---

[1] Palmer's *Desert Of The Exodus*, I., 90.

[2] Burckhardt's *Bed. U. Wahaby*, p. 214, note.

[3] Lane's *Modern Egyptians*, II., 293.

[4] Garnett's *Women of Turkey and Their Folk-Lore* ("Christian Women"), p. 239.

[5] Rodd's *Customs and Lore of Modern Greece*, p. 101.

east Central Africa: "On reaching the bridegroom's house a low-caste man sacrifices a goat or sheep on the threshold; and the bride steps over it"; and again when the bridegroom returns from his devotions at a neighboring *masjid* (a place of public prayer) to claim his bride, as he reaches his threshold, "another goat is sacrificed, and he steps over it in the same way as his bride."[1] Again the bridegroom himself brings the bride from her father's hut to his own, accompanied by young men and maidens dancing and singing. "On reaching the new hut, the bride holds a goat or sheep in the doorway, while the bridegroom cuts its throat in the orthodox manner with his *jambia* (long knife). The bride dips her finger in the blood, smears it on her forehead . . . and then enters the *guri*, stepping over the blood. The bridegroom follows her, also stepping over the blood, and is accompanied by some of his nearest male relatives."[2]

There are traces of such customs, also, among the natives of South Africa[3], and elsewhere.

Besides the bloody sacrifices at the threshold, in the marriage ceremony, there are, in different countries, various forms of making offerings at the threshold, and of surmounting obstacles at that point, as an accompaniment of the wedding covenant. All these point to the importance and sanctity of the threshold and doorway in the primitive mind.

---

[1] Capt. King's "Notes" in London *Folk-Lore Journal*, VI.,121,123.

[2] Capt. King's "Notes" in London *Folk-Lore Journal*, VI.,121,123.

[3] Shooter's *Kafirs of Natal*, pp.71-78; and Anderson's *Lake Ngami*, p. 220f.

A bride, in portions of Upper Syria, on reaching her husband's house, is lifted up so that she can press against the door-lintel a piece of dough, prepared for the purpose, and handed to her at that time. This soft dough, thus pressed against the plastered or clay wall, adheres firmly, and is left there as long as it will remain. The open hand of the bride stamps the dough as it is fixed in place, and in some cases the finger points are pricked before the stamping, so that the blood will appear as a sign manual on the cake of dough.[1]

When a bride reaches the door of her husband's house, among the fellaheen of Palestine, a jar of water is placed on her head. She must call on the name of God as she crosses the threshold; and, at the same moment, her husband strikes the jar from her head, and causes the water to flow as a libation.[2]

Among the Wallachians there is a marriage rite, said to be of Latin origin, because there was a similar rite among the old Latins. The Wallachian bride is borne on horseback, with an accompanying procession, to the house of the bridegroom. "At the moment when the betrothed maiden dismounts from her steed, and is about to cross the threshold, they present to her butter, or sometimes honey, and with this she smears the door-posts."[3]

---

[1] On the testimony of a native eye-witness. See, also, Conder's *Heth and Moab*, p. 285.

[2] See article by P.J. Baldensperger, in *Quarterly Statement* of Palestine Exploration Fund for April, 1894, p. 136.

[3] Henzey's *Le Monte Olympe et L'Acarnanie*, p. 278.

An observer says of this rite: "For the same reason among the Latins, the word for wife, *uxpr*, originally *unxor*, was derived from the verb *ungere*, 'to anoint,' because the maidens when they reached the threshold of their future husbands, were similarly accustomed to anoint the door-posts." In support of this fanciful etymology, old-time commentators on Terence and Virgil are cited;[1] which shows, at least, that this ceremony at the threshold of the husband's home has long been recognized as of vital importance in the marriage contract and relation.

It is customary, among the Greeks in Turkey, for the mother of the bridegroom, as he leaves his home to go for his bride on the morning of the wedding, to lay across his pathway a girdle, over which he steps, and to pour a libation of water before him.[2]

In the Morea, in the vicinity of Sparta, it is said that, when the bride is brought to her new home, the mother of the bridegroom "stands waiting at the door, holding a glass of honey and water in her hand. From this glass of honey and water the bride must drink . . . while the lintel of the door is smeared with the remainder . . . in the meantime one of the company breaks a pomegranate on the threshold."[3] In Rhodes, when the newly married couple enter the doorway of their new home, the husband, "dips his finger in

---

[1] See citations from Donatus, on the "Hecyra" of Terence, I., 2, 60, and Servius on Virgil's "Aeneid," IV. 459, in Heuzey's *Le Monte Olympe et Acarnanie*, p.278; also, Marquardt's *Privatleben Der Romer*, p. 53.

[2] Garnett's *Women of Turkey* ("Christian Women"), p. 82.

[3] Rodd's *Customs and Lore of Modern Greece*, p. 95f.

a cup of honey, and traces a cross over the door . . . A pomegranate is placed on the threshold, which the young husband crushes with his foot as he enters, followed by his wife, over whom the wedding guests throw corn and cotton seeds and orange flower water."[1]

On Skarpanto (Carpathos), an island lying between Rhodes and Crete, when the bridegroom reaches the door of the bride's house "he is greeted by the mother of the bride, who touches the nape of his neck with a censer containing incense . . . She further gives him a present called *embatikon*, —that is to say, 'the gift of in-going,' —and then places on the threshold a rug or blanket folded, with a stick resting on one of the corners. The bridegroom advances his right foot, breaks the stick and passes in."[2]

Among the Morlacchi, in Dalmatia, it is, or was, a custom for a bride to kneel and kiss the threshold of her husband's home, before crossing it for the first time. Her mother-in-law, or some near relative of her husband, at the same time presented her with a sieve full of different kinds of grain, nuts, and small fruits, which the bride scattered behind her back as she passed in.[3]

It is a custom in portions of Russia, when the bride is about to leave her father's home to meet the bridegroom, for the friends to appear at the door, and request that the bride be brought to them. "After their request has been many times repeated, the 'princess' [as the bride is called]

[1] Rodd's *Customs and Lore of Modern Greece*, p. 99f.

[2] Ibid., p.102.

[3] Wood's *Wedding Day in All Ages and Countries*, II., 46.

appears, attended by her relatives and attendants, but stops short at the door. Again the bridegroom's friends demand the bride, but are told first to 'cleanse the threshold; then will the young princess cross the threshold.'" Thereupon gifts are made by the bridegroom's friend, and the bride crosses the threshold to go to the bridegroom.[1]

Among the Mordvins (or, Mordevins), a Finnish people on the Volga, there are various customs in connection with marriage, tending to confirm the idea that the threshold is the household altar. In a ceremony of betrothal, with a conference over the terms of dowry, a prayer is offered to the "goddess of the homestead," and the "goddess of the dwelling house;" "the girl's father then cuts off the corner of a loaf of bread with three slashes of a knife, salts it, and places it under the threshold, where the Penates are believed to frequent. This is called the 'gods' portion.' " Bread and salt are factors in a sacred covenant, and their proffer to the household gods, at the threshold altar, would, seem to be an invitation to those gods to be a party to the new marriage covenant. Again, after the terms of betrothal are agreed on, there is the feast of "hand-striking," or ratification of the betrothal. On that occasion also the "gods' portion" is offered; and "a little brandy is spilt under the threshold. Bread and salt are once more placed under the threshold by the bride's father, who carries it from the table to the household altar "on the point of the knife—under no circum-

---

[1] See Ralston's *Songs of the Russian People*, p.277f.

stances in his hands."[1]

A custom of strewing the threshold of the home of a new-married couple prevailed in Holland until recent times.[2] This was obviously a form of offering at the household altar.

On the evening before the marriage ceremony, in the rural districts and smaller towns of Northern Germany, the boys and girls, and others in the neighborhood, are accustomed to appear at the door of the bride's house, and smash on the threshold earthen pots and jars, with loud cries of joy. "Sometimes, whole car-loads of broken pottery have to be removed from the door the next morning." And when the young couple return to their home, after the ceremony at the church, poor boys and girls are accustomed to stretch a colored cord across the door of the house, to prevent a passage over the threshold, unless the bridegroom throws a handful of small coins among those who bar the way.[3]

Traces of the sacredness of the threshold altar seem to exist in the wedding ceremonies in villages on the coast of Aberdeenshire, Scotland. "After the marriage is solemnized . . . the bride's guests are entertained at her home, and the bridegroom's at his . . . When the bride returns to her father's house, after the marriage, broken bread of various sorts is thrown over her before she enters. The same ceremony is gone through with the bridegroom at his

---

[1] See "Marriage Customs of the Mordvins," in London *Folk-Lore*, I., 422-427; also P. von Stenin, in *Globus* LXV., 181-183.

[2] Wood's *Wedding Day in All Ages and Countries*, II., 13.

[3] On the testimony of Dr. H. V. Hilprecht.

father's door."[1]

When a girl among the Sea Dyaks of Borneo is married, the wedding takes place at her house. The marriage rite includes the erecting an altar before the door of the house, and placing on it an offering of prepared areca-nut, covered with a red cloth, the color of blood. The families of the bride and the groom then partake of that offering in covenant conclave.[2]

A lover, among the Woolwas, in Central America, when wooing a bride, would bring a deer's carcass, and a bundle of firewood, and deposit it outside of her house door. If she accepted these, and took them over the threshold, it was a betrothal.[3]

The covenant seemed to consist in the reaching across the threshold and accepting a proffered offering in a spirit of loving agreement.

Among the Towkas, in the same part of the world, a bridegroom would go with his friends to the home of his bride, carrying a bundle of gifts for her. Sitting down outside of the door, he would call on her family to open to him. There being no response, music would then be tried by his friends. At this the door would be opened just far enough for him to put a gift inside over the threshold. One by one his gifts would be passed in, in this way, while the door opened wider and wider. When the last gift was over the threshold, the lover would spring within, and, seizing

[1] Walter Gregor in London *Folk-Lore Journal*, I., 119f.

[2] St. John's *Life in the Forests of the Far East.*, I., 62.

[3] See Bancroft's *Native Races*, I., 603.

the bride, would carry her across the threshold, and take her to a temporary hut erected within a charmed circle near by, while his friends guarded him from intrusion.[1]

And thus, in various ways, among widely different primitive peoples, the marriage customs go to show that the home threshold cannot be passed except by overcoming a barrier of some kind, and making an offering, bloody or bloodless, at this primal family altar. An essential part of the covenant of union is a halting at, and then passing over, the threshold of the new home, with an accompanying sacrifice.

4. STEPPING, OR BEING LIFTED, ACROSS THE THRESHOLD

Even more widespread and prominent than the customs of offering blood, or of making a libation, or of overcoming a special barrier, at the threshold, or of anointing or stamping the posts or lintel of the doorway as a sign of the covenant, at the time of a marriage, and as a part of the ceremony, is the habit of causing the bride to cross the threshold with care, without stepping upon it. The custom is of well-nigh world-wide observance, and it has attracted the attention of anthropologists and students of primitive customs. A favorite method of explaining it has been by calling it a survival of the practice of "marriage by capture"; but this is nothing more than an unscientific guess, in defiance of the truth that persistent popular customs have

[1] See Bancroft's *Native Races.*, I., 732-734.

their origin in a sentiment, and not in a passing historic practice. The earliest mentions of this custom, of the bride's crossing the threshold without stepping on it, show it as a voluntary religious rite; and there are traces of its recognition in this light from the earliest times until now.

In the Vedic Sutras, or the sacrificial rules of the ancient Hindoo literature, it is specifically declared that a bride, on entering her husband's home, shall step across the threshold, and not upon it. She is not lifted over the door-sill, but she voluntarily crosses it. Thus it is said: When (the bridegroom with his bride) has come to his house, he says to her, 'Cross (the threshold) with thy right foot first; do not stand on the threshold.'"[1] In this ancient ceremony, grains of rice are poured on the heads of the bridegroom and his bride.[2] This modern custom has, therefore, a very early origin. And again: "He makes her enter the house (which she does) with her right foot. And she does not stand on the threshold."[3]

Putting the right foot forward seems to be a matter of importance in various primitive religions. "Put your right foot first" is a maxim ascribed to Pythagoras.[4] In his description of the proportions of a temple, the Roman architect Vitruvius said: "The number of steps in front

---

[1] "Grihya-Sutras," or Rules of Vedic Domestic Cerremonies, in *Sacred Books of the East,* XXX., 193

[2] *Ibid.*

[3] *Ibid.,* p. 263.

[4] *Fragmenta Philosophorum Graecorum* (ed. Mullach). I., 510.

should always be odd, since, in that case, the right foot, which begins the ascent, will be that which first alights on the landing of the temple."[1] A Muhammadan is always careful to put his right foot first in crossing over the threshold of a mosk."[2]

Among the Albanians, when the bride is taken to the home of the bridegroom, accompanied by the *vlam,* or "the friend of the bridegroom," it is said that "particular care is taken that the threshold should be crossed with the right foot foremost."[3] Here, as in India, the crossing of the threshold is a voluntary act. The bride is not lifted over, but crosses of her own accord. If she be veiled, the lifting is a necessity.

In Madagascar, "on entering a house, especially; a royal house, it is improper to use the left foot on first stepping into it. One must 'put one's best (or right) foot foremost'"[4]

The bride, in Upper Syria, is sometimes carried across the threshold of the bridegroom's house by friends of the bridegroom.[5] She, of course, is veiled.

When the bride reaches the outer gate of her husband's residence, in Egypt, the bridegroom meets her, enveloped as

---

[1] Gwilt's *Architecture of Marcus Vitruvius Pollio*, p. 80.

[2] See Hughes's *Dictionary of Islam*, art."Masjad;" also Lane's *Modern Egyptians,* I., 105; and Conder's *Heth and Moab*, p. 203f.

[3] Rodd's *Customs and Lore of Modern Greece*, p. 104.

[4] Sibree, on "Malagasy Folk-Lore and Popular Superstition" in London *Folk-Lore Record,* II., p. 37.

[5] As told me by a native eye-witness.

she is in her cashmere shawl, clasps her in his arms, and carries her across the threshold, and up to the doorway of the female apartments.[1]

In portions of Abyssinia, the bridegroom carries his bride from her home to his, bearing her across the threshold as he enters his house.[2]

So, also, it is among the more primitive tribes in West Africa. The bride is carried over the threshold in a rude chair, or on the shoulders of her friends, into her new home.[3]

There are traces of a similar custom in the marriage ceremonies of ancient Assyria.[4]

Again, it is said to be found among the Khonds of Orissa,[5] the Tatars,[6] and the Eskimos.[7]

---

[1] Burckhardt's *Arabic Proverbs*, p. 137f.

[2] Bruce's "Travels," VII., 07 (ed.1804); cited in McLennan's *Studies In Ancient History*, p. 188.

[3] On the testimony of a colored clergyman from Liberia.

[4] See Maspero's *Life in Ancient Egypt and Assyria*, p. 232.

[5] Campbell's "Personal Narrative;" cited in McLennan's *Studies in Ancient History*, p. 14.

[6] Pinkerton's *Collection*, VI., 183; cited in Ibid., p. 177.

[7] Hayes's "Open Polar Sea," p. 432; cited in Lubbock's *Origin of Civilization* (Am.ed.), p. 78.

In ancient Greece[1] and in ancient Rome[2] the lifting of the bride over the threshold of her new home was an important part of the marriage ceremony. Classic writers had their explanations of this custom, as certain modern anthropologists have theirs, but the origin of the ceremony was earlier than they imagined.

In unchanging China the use of fire on the threshold altar, in connection with the marriage ceremony, is continued to the present day. The bride is borne in a sedan-chair to the house of the bridegroom, accompanied by a procession of friends and musicians, "On arriving at the portal of the house, the bridegroom taps the door of the sedan-chair with his fan, and in response, the instructress of matrimony, who prompts every act of the bride, opens the door and hands out the still enshrouded young lady, who is carried bodily over a pan of lighted charcoal, or a red-hot coulter laid on the threshold, while at the same moment a servant offers for her acceptance some rice and preserved prunes."[3]

Again, it is burning straw that is thrown upon the door-sill, and is half extinguished before the Chinese bride is led to step across it. The instructress says at this point:

---

[1] Rous' *Archaeologia Attica*, Lib.IV., cap.7.

[2] See "Roman Questions," Q.29, in Goodwin's *Plutarch's Morais*, II., 220f; also Godwyn's *Rom. Hist. Anthol.*, Lib. II., #2; citation of authorities in Becker's *Gallus*, p. 161, and in Marquardt's *Privatleben der Romer*, I.,53f.

[3] Douglas' *Society in China*, p. 201. See, also, Williams' *Middle Kingdom*, I., 790; Gray's *China*, I., 205; and "Marriage Ceremonies of the Manchus," in London *Folk-Lore*, I., 487.

"Now, fair young bride, the smoke bestride;
This year have joy, next year a boy."[1]

Fire, like blood, stands for life in the primitive mind; and fire, like blood, has its place on the altar. Indeed, as the first threshold altar was the hearthstone, it was the place on the altar. Indeed, as the first threshold altar was the hearthstone, it was the place of the household fire. The sacredness of the domestic fire is recognized in all the Hindoo religious literature; and a Hindoo couple, on beginning their married life, must have a care to enter a new home bringing their sacred altar fire with them.[2] In ancient Greece, the mother of the bride accompanied her daughter to the threshold of her new home, bearing a flaming torch "kindled at the parental hearth, according to custom immemorial."[3] A torch was similarly borne in the Roman marriage ceremonies.[4] This custom is referred to in the term "hymen's torch," or the "nuptial torch." "In Cicero's time, they did not distinguish the hearth-fire from the Penates, nor the Penates from the Lares."[5] The bride in

---

[1] Adele M. Fielde's *Corner of Cathay*, p. 39.

[2] "Grihya-Sutras," or Rules of Vedic Domestic Ceremonies, in *Sacred Books of the East*, XXX., 193,201.

[3] Guhl and Koner's *Life of the Greeks and Romans*, p. 192.

[4] See "Roman Questions," Q.1,2, in Goodwin's *Plutarch's Morals*, I., 204; also authorities cited in Becker's *Gallus*, p. 162f., and Marquardt's *Privatleben Der Romer*, I.,53f.

[5] See Coulange's *Ancient City*, pp. 29-41, 55-58, with citations.

India, in China, in Greece, and in Rome, worshiped at the altar-fire of her new home.

A connecting link between the altar fire and the nuptial torch is found in a marriage custom of the Erza, of the Mordvins, in Russia. On the eve of the wedding day the bridegroom's family make ready for the bride. "A thick candle, and several thinner ones, have . . . been made ready for the occasion. The bridegroom's father lights the smaller ones before the holy pictures [in use in families of the Greek Church], but sets up the large one on the threshold. It is called 'the house candle'" The father then prays for the new couple.[1]

A survival of an ancient Slavic custom, of covenanting together by crossing together an altar fire, would also seem to exist in Russia in the practices of young people at the "Midsummer Day" festival. A Russian writer says of these festivals: "More than once have I had an opportunity of being present at these nightly meetings, held at the end of June, in commemoration of a heathen divinity. They usually take place close to a river or pond; large fires are lighted, and over them young couples, bachelors and unmarried girls, jump barefoot."[2]

There is a custom of wooing among the Moksha, of the Mordvins, that brings the threshold-altar idea into prominence. The parents of the wooer first make gifts, at

---

[1] See "Marriage Customs of the Mordvins," in London *Folk-Lore*, I., 437. See also the reference to burning incense on the threshold in Tuscany, at p. 17f., supra.

[2] See Kowalewsky's "Marriage among the Early Slavs," in London *Folk-Lore*, I., 467.

their home, to the household goddesses, "These gifts consist of dough figures of domestic animals, which are placed under the threshold of the house and of the outside gate, while prayer is made to the goddesses and to deceased ancestors. The father [of the bridegroom] then cuts off a corner of a loaf placed on the table, and at the time of the offering scoops out the inside and fills it with honey. At midnight he drives in profound secrecy to the house of the bride elect, places the honeyed bread on the gatepost [of her house], strikes the window with his whip, and shouts: '*Seta!* I, *Veshnak Masakoff*, make a match between thy daughter and my son *Uru*. 'Take the honeyed bread from thy gate-post, and pray.' "[1] The images of domestic animals would here seem to stand for the slaughtered animals formerly offered at the threshold altar; and the linking of the altars of the two homes by offerings and prayer would seem to indicate the desire for a sacred covenant. When the bride is received at the bridegroom's house, a notch is cut "with an ax in the door-post to mark the arrival of a new addition to the family."

Among the Erza, of the same province, the bride, on the day of "the girl's feast," preceding her marriage, "takes mould [earth] from under the threshold [of her parental home] with her finger-tips, and thrusts it into her bosom, as she goes out to seek a farewell blessing from her friends. In the bridegroom's home, meanwhile, a lighted candle is placed on the threshold of the door; and, in some regions,

---

[1] From "Marriage Customs of the Mordvins," in London *Folk-Lore*, I., 423, 447.

when he and his friends go to the bride's house to bring her to his home, he and they are met at the door by her parents with the covenanting bread and salt, and the words, "Be welcome, come within." As the bride is borne out of her old home to go to her new one, she and her party "all halt and bow to the gate, for there, or in the courtyard, is the abode of the god that protects the dwelling-place. The following prayer is made to him: '*Kardas Sarks*, the nourisher, god of the house, do not abandon her that is about to depart; always be near her just as thou art here.'" When she reaches her new home, she is carried (over the threshold), in the arms of some of her party, into the house of the bridegroom, carrying a lighted candle.[1]

The custom survived in portions of Scotland, as recently as the beginning of this century, of lifting a bride-over the threshold, or the first step of the door. A cake of bread, prepared for the occasion, was, at the same time, broken by the bridegroom's mother over the head of the bride. The bride was then led directly to the hearth, and the poker and tongs, and sometimes the broom, were put into her hands "as symbols of her office and duty."

Lifting the bride over the threshold has been practiced in recent times, in England, Ireland, and the United States.[2]

Both bride and bridegroom were carried, on the shoulders of their elders, across the threshold of their new home, and laid on their bridal bed, in the marriage ceremonies of

---

[1] From "Marriage Customs of the Mordvins," in London *Folk-Lore*, I., 434-443.

[2] Napier's *Folk-lore in the West of Scotland,* p. 51; also Wood's *Wedding Day in All Ages and Countries*, II., 59f.

some of the tribes of Central America. And again, the
bridegroom carried his bride in this way.[1] In either case, it
was the crossing of the threshold without stepping on it that
was the thing aimed at.

5. LAYING FOUNDATIONS IN BLOOD.

In the building of a house, as a new home, the prominence given to the laying of the threshold, or to its dedi-
cating by blood, is another indication, or outcome of its
altar-like sacredness. In Upper Syria a sacrifice is often
made at the beginning of the building of a new house, and
again at the first crossing of its threshold. "When a new
house is built," among the Metawilch, "the owner will not
reside in it until, with certain formalities, a black hen has
been carried several times round the house and slaughtered
within the door," as if in covenant dedication of the house.[2]

Among the Copts in Egypt, when the threshold of a
new house is laid, the owner slaughters a sheep or a goat on
the threshold, and steps over the blood, as if in covenant for
himself and his household with Him to whom all blood, as
life, belongs. Then he divides the sacrificed victim among
his neighbors; and they in turn come and step across the
blood on the threshold, invoking as they do so a blessing on
the new house and its owner, while coming into covenant

---

[1] See Bancroft's *Native Races*, I., 662,703,730-734.

[2] On the testimony of the Rev. William Ewing, a missionary in Palestine.

with him.[1]

The foundation-stone of a new building is, in a sense, the threshold of that structure. Hence to lay the foundations in blood is to proffer blood at the threshold. Traces of this custom are to be found in the practices or the legends of peoples wellnigh all the world over.[2] Apparently the earlier sacrifices were of human beings.[3] Later they were of animals substituted for persons. The idea seems to have been that he who covenanted by blood with God, or with the gods, when his house, or his city, was builded, was guarded, together with his household, while he and they were dwellers there; but, if he failed to proffer a threshold sacrifice, his first-born, or the first person who crossed the bloodless threshold, would be claimed by the ignored or defied deity.

There is, indeed, a suggestion of this idea in the curse pronounced by Joshua, when he destroyed the doomed city of Jericho, against him who should rebuild its walls, he not being in covenant with and obedient to the Lord. "Cursed be the man before the Lord, that riseth up and buildeth this city Jericho: with the loss of his firstborn shall he lay the foundation thereof, and with the loss of his youngest son

---

[1] A daughter of a native Copt described to me this ceremony, as she witnessed it at the building of her father's house in 1878. He was formerly a Coptic priest, but was now a Protestant Christian.

[2] See Tylor's *Primitive Culture*, I., 104-108.

[3] Strack's *Der Blutaberglaube*, p. 68.

shall he set up the gates of it."[1] A later record tells of the fulfillment of this curse. It says of the reign of Ahab: "In his days did Hiel the Bethel-ite build Jericho; he laid the foundation thereof with the loss of Abiram his firstborn, and set up the gates thereof with the loss of his youngest son Segub; according to the word of the Lord, which he spake by the hand of Joshua the son of Nun."[2]

Human sacrifices, in order to furnish blood at the foundations of a house, or of a public structure, have been continued down to recent times, or to the present, in some portions of the world; and there are indications in popular tradition that they were frequent in a not remote past.

It is said that at the building of Scutari, in Asia Minor, "the workmen were engaged on its fortifications for three years, but the walls would not stand. Then they protested that the only possible way to succeed was to lay under or in them a living human being. They accordingly laid hold of a young woman who brought them dinner; and immured her."[3]

According to a story in China, when the bridge leading to the site of St. John's College, in Shanghai, was in process of building, an official present took off his shoes, as indicating his rank, and threw them into the stream, in order to stay the current, and enable the workmen to lay the foundations. Finding this unavailing, he took off his

---

[1] Josh. 6:26.

[2] I Kings 16:34.

[3] See article "On Kirk-Grims" in *the Cornhill Magazine* for February, 1887, p. 196.

garments and threw them in. Finally he threw himself in, and as his life went out the workmen were enabled to go on with their building. To this day the belief is general that structure stands fast because of this sacrifice.[1]

"When the walls of Algiers were built of blocks of concrete (by Muhammadans), in the sixteenth century, a Christian captive named Geronimo was placed in one of the blocks and the rampart built over and about him. Since the French occupation of Algiers a subsidence in the wall led to an examination of the blocks, and one was found to have given way. It was removed, and the cast of Geronimo was discovered in the block. The body had gone to dust, and the superincumbent weight had crushed in the stone sarcophaghus."[2]

A story told among the Danes is, that "many years ago, when the ramparts were being raised round Copenhagen, the wall always sank, so that it was not possible to get it to stand firm. They therefore took a little innocent girl, placed her in a chair by a table, and give her playthings and sweetmeats. While she thus sat enjoying herself, twelve masons built an arch over her, which, when completed, they covered with earth to the sound of drums and trumpets. By this process the walls were made solid."[3]

"Thuringian legend declares that to make the castle of Liebenstein fast and impregnable, a child was bought for

---

[1] On the testimony of a native Chinese clergyman.

[2] See article "On Kirk-Grims" in *the Cornhill Magazine* for February,1887.

[3] See article "On Kirk Grims" in *the Cornhill Magazine* for February, 1887, p. 191.

hard money of its mother, and walled in. It was eating a cake while the masons were at work, the story goes, and it cried, 'Mother, I see thee still;' then later, 'Mother, I see thee a little still;' and as they put in the last stone, 'Mother, now I see thee no more.'"[1]

A similar story is told of a Slavic town on the Danube. A plague devastated it, and it was determined to build it anew, with a new citadel. "Acting on the advice of their wisest men, they sent out messengers before sunrise one morning in all directions, with orders to seize upon the first living creature they should meet. The victim proved to be a child (*Dyetina*, archaic form of *Ditya*), who was buried alive under the foundation-stone of the new citadel. The city was on that account called Dyetinets [or Detinetz], a name since applied to any citadel."[2]

It is even said that "when, a few years ago, the Bridge Gate of the Bremen city walls was demolished, the skeleton of a child was found imbedded in the foundations."[3]

A Scottish legend tells that St. Columba found himself unable to build a cathedral on the island of Iona unless he would secure its stability and safety by the blood of a human sacrifice. Thereupon he took his companion, Oran, and buried him alive at the foundations of the structure, having

---

[1] Tylor's *Primitive Culture*, I., 104f.

[2] Ralston's *Songs of the Russian People,* p. 128.

[3] See article "on Kirk Grims" in *The Cornhill Magazine* for February, 1887, p. 191

no trouble after that.[1]

And it is said that under the walls of the only two round towers of the ancient Irish examined, human skeletons were found buried.[2]

Until the transfer of Alaska to the United States, in 1867, by the Russian government, human sacrifices at the foundation of a new house were common in that portion of America. The ceremonies are thus described by one familiar with them: "The rectangular space for the building is . . . cleared, a spot for the fireplace designated, and four holes dug, wherein the corner posts are to be set . . . A slave, either man or woman who has been captured in war or is even a descendant of such a slave, is blindfolded and compelled to lie down face uppermost in the place selected for the fireplace [the site of the domestic altar]. A sapling is then cut, laid across the throat of the slave, and, at a given signal, the two nearest relatives of the host sit upon the respective ends of the sapling, thereby choking the unhappy wretch to death. But the corner posts must receive their baptism; so four slaves are blindfolded, and one is forced to stand in each post-hold, when, at a given signal, a blow on the forehead is dealt with a peculiar club ornamented with the host's coat of arms." It is said that even to the present time, on the building of a house in Alaska, "the same ceremonies are enacted, with the exception of the sacrifices,

---

[1] See Gomme's article on "Traditions Connected with Buildings," in *the Antiquary*, III.,11.

[2] See Coote's "A Building Superstition," in London *Folk-Lore Journal*, I., 22f.

which are prevented by the United States authorities."[1]

In Hindoostan, Burmah, Tennasserin, Borneo, Japan, Galam, Yarriba, Polynesia, and elsewhere, there are modern survivals of this foundation-laying in blood.[2] It would seem, indeed, to have been wellnigh universal as a primitive usage.

Popular ballads give other indications of such customs, in various lands. "In a song, of which there are several versions, of the building of the bridge of Arta, it is told how the bridge fell down as fast as it was built, until at last the master-builder dreamed a dream that it would only stand if his own wife were buried alive in the foundations. He therefore sends for her, bidding her dress in festival attire, and then finds an excuse to make her descend into the central pile, whereupon they heap the earth over her, and thus the bridge stands fast."[3]

"In another song the same story is told of the Bridge of Tricha, with the difference only that it is a little bird that whispers in the architect's ear how the pile may be made to stand. A similar superstition connected with the building of the monastery Curtea de Argest, in Wallachia, forms the subject of a fine poem by the Roumanian poet Alexandri."[4]

There is an indication of a like custom among the

---

[1] See W. G. Chase's "Notes from Alaska," in *Journal of American Folk-Lore,* VI., 51.

[2] See Tylor's *Primitive Culture,* I., 104-108.

[3] Rodd's *Customs and Lore of Modern Greece,* p. 168f.

[4] *Ibid.*

Vlachs in Turkey, as shown in their folk-poetry. The ballad of the "Monastery of Argis" tells of such an incident, in which the master-builder Manoli plays a part.[1]

Various substitutes for human offerings at the laying of a foundation-stone, or a threshold, have been adopted in different countries. Thus, in modern Greece, "after the ground has been cleared for the foundations of a new house, the future owner, his family, and the workmen attend, together with the *pappas* [the priest] in full canonicals, accompanied by incense, holy water, and all due accessories. A prayer is said, and those present are as-persed, and the site is sprinkled with the consecrated water. Then a fowl or a lamb, which you have noticed lying near with the feet tied together, is taken by one of the workmen, killed and decapitated, the *pampas* standing by all the while, and even giving directions; the blood is then smeared on the foundation-stone, in the fulfillment of the popular adage that 'there must be blood in the foundation.'"[2]

The modern Greek term for this ceremony, *stoicheio-nein*, would seem to indicate a sacrifice to the deity of the threshold, or the foundation.

"The Bulgarians, it is said, when laying a house foun-dation, take a thread, and measure the shadow of some casual passer-by. The measure is then buried under the foundation-stone and it is expected that the man whose shadow has been thus treated will soon become but a shade himself . . . Sometimes a victim is put to death on the

---

[1] Garnett's *Women of Turkey* (Christian Women"), p.22.

[2] Rodd's *Customs and Lore of Modern Greece*, p. 148.

occasion; the foundations being sprinkled with the blood of a fowl, or a lamb, or some other species of scapegoat." [1]

Among the Russian peasants the idea prevails that the building of a new house "is apt to be followed by the death of the head of the family for which the new dwelling is constructed, or that the member of the family who is the first to enter it will soon die. In accordance with a custom of great antiquity, the oldest member of a migrating household enters the new house first; and in many places, as, for instance, in the Government of Archangel, some animal is killed and buried on the spot on which the first log or stone is laid." [2]

The "upper corner" of a house, in Russia, is peculiarly sacred, having even more honor than the doorway threshold in the ordinary home. Yet this upper corner seems to be in a sense the real threshold, or foundation corner, of the building. A cock is the ordinary victim sacrificed "on the spot which a projected house is to cover." The head of this cock is buried "exactly where the 'upper corner' of the building is to stand. And this corner is thenceforward a sacred corner. Opposite to it is the stove. It is called the "great" and the "beautiful" corner. The family meal is eaten before it, and every one who enters the cottage makes obeisance toward it. Formerly ancestral images are supposed to have been in that corner, and now holy pictures

---

[1] See Ralston's *Songs of the Russian People*, p.126.

[2] *Ibid.*, p.127.

are there.[1] It would seem to be in accordance with this idea that the foundation-stone, or threshold, of a new building, which in civilized lands is now laid with imposing ceremonies, is known as the "cornerstone." Yet the "cornerstone" of a modern building is sometimes at the corner of the central doorway.[2]

It is worthy of note that in ancient Egypt the one door of an ordinary dwelling-house was placed at one side, or end, of the front wall, and not in the center; so that the cornerstone of the building was literally a portion of the threshold.[3] The same was true of many an old-time New England house; the "front door" was at the left-hand side (as one approached the house) of the gable end. Thus the threshold of the door was often the cornerstone.

Ancient Romans were accustomed to place statues and images, instead of living persons, under the foundations of their buildings, as has been shown by recent researches in and about Rome.[4] In one instance, where a fine statue of colossal size and in perfect preservation was unearthed, at the foundations of a convent which was being enlarged, "by order of the monks, it was buried again," as if in deference to the primitive belief that it was essential to the stability of

---

[1] Ralston's *Songs of the Russian People,* p. 135f

[2] This is the case with the Church House in Philadelphia, - the "cornerstone" of which was laid while this page was writing.

[3] See Erman's *Life in Ancient Egypt,* p.175.

[4] See Coote's "A Building Superstition," in London *Folk-Lore Journal,* I., 22.

the structure.[1]

There is a Swedish tradition "that under the altar in the first Christian churches a lamb was usually buried, which imparted security and duration to the edifice."[2] And, "according to Danish accounts, a lamb was buried under every altar, and a living horse was laid in every churchyard before a human corpse was laid in it. Both lamb and horse are to be seen occasionally in the church - or grave-yard, and betoken death. Under other houses pigs and hens were buried alive."[3]

A new sacrificial stone, or altar of sacrifice, laid on the summit of a Mexican temple, in 1512, was consecrated by Montezuma by the blood of more than twelve thousand captives.[4]

When the new railroad was built between Jaffa and Jerusalem, a few years ago, there were sacrifices of sheep at its beginning. And there were similar sacrifices at the foundations of the Turkish building, at the Columbian Exposition at Chicago.

In all these facts or legends, blood on the threshold of the building, in the foundation-stones of the structure, is shown to have been deemed an essential factor in a covenant with, or in propitiation of, the deity of the place.

---

[1] Lanciani's *Ancient Rome in the Light of Recent Discoveries*, p. 225f.

[2] See article "On Kirk-Grims" in *The Cornhill Magazine* for February, 1887, p. 192.

[3] *Ibid.*, p. 195.

[4] See Bancroft's *Native Races,* V., 471.

6. APPEALS AT THE ALTAR

Because the threshold is recognized as an altar, nearness to the altar is nearness to God, or to the gods worshiped at that altar. Hence appeals are made and justice is sought at the gate, or at the threshold, as in the presence of deity.

To present one's self at the tent doorway, or to lay hold of the supports, or cords, at the entrance of an Arab's "house of hair," is recognized as an ever-effective appeal for hospitality in the East. Even an enemy can thus secure the protection of the home sanctuary.[1]

In the excavation of Tell-el-Hesy, in Southwestern Palestine, supposed to cover the remains of ancient Lachish,[2] Dr. Petrie discovered various ornamented door-jambs. In one case a simple volute on pilaster slab suggested to Dr. Petrie "a ram's horn nailed up against a wooden post;" and "he sees in this the origin of the type of the 'horns of the altar,'[3] so often mentioned in temple architecture."[4] If Dr. Petrie be correct in this thought, the horns of the altar were first of all at the house doorway, above the threshold altar.

---

[1] See Trumbull's *Studies in Oriental Social Life,* pp. 98, 112-131.

[2] See Josh. 10:3-35; 12:11; 1539; II Kings 14:19; 18:14-19,etc.

[3] See, for example, I Kings 2:28.

[4] See Bliss's *Mound of Many Cities,* p. 77f.

One of the fundamental laws of the Afghans makes it incumbent on a host to "shelter and protect anyone who in extremity may flee to his threshold, and seek an asylum under his roof." Property or life must be sacrificed in his behalf, if need be. "As soon as you have crossed the threshold of an Afghan you are sacred to him, though you were his deadly foe, and he will give up his own life to save yours." A favorite poem of the Afghan, entitled, "Adam Khan and Durkhani," tells of a son who killed his father because that father had betrayed a refugee who sought the sanctuary of his threshold. And all Afghans honor the memory of that son.[1]

Among the Arabs of the Syrian desert, when a man would leave his own tribe and join himself to another, he takes a lamb or a goat with him, and presents himself at the entrance of the tent of the shaykh of the tribe he would find a home in. Slaying the animal there, and allowing its blood to run out on the ground at the threshold of the tent, he makes his appeal to the shaykh to accept him as a member of his tribe, or as a son by adoption. And this appeal has peculiar force, as a voice by blood.[2]

When a man among these tribes is in peril of his life, pursued by an enemy, he can similarly make an appeal for sanctuary at the threshold altar of a shaykh's tent, with a like outpouring of the blood of an animal brought by him; and protection must be granted him by the shaykh. It is as

[1] See "Afghan Life in Afghan Songs," in Darmesteter's *Selected Essays*, p. 117.

[2] On the testimony of a native Syrian of wide experience in the region referred to.

though he had laid hold of the "horns of the altar." So, again, when a man would be reconciled with an enemy who has cause for bitter hostility, he goes to the tent of that enemy and sacrifices an animal at the threshold, with an appeal for forgiveness. This offering of a threshold sacrifice secures his safety.

In other portions of Arabia this same idea finds a different but similar expression. "With bare and shaven head the offender appears at the door of the injured person, holding a knife in each hand, and, reciting a formula provided for the purpose, strikes his head several times with the sharp blades. Then drawing his hands over his bloody scalp, he wipes them on the door-post. The other must then come out and cover the suppliant's head with a shawl [covering the offense, in covering the offender], after which he kills a sheep, and they sit down together at a feast of reconciliation."[1]

A record on a Babylonian clay tablet, of the twenty-eighth year of Nebuchadrezzar affirms that "on the second day of the month of Ab" a certain "Imbi'a shall bring his witness to the gate of the house of the chief Bel-iddin, and let him testify "as to a certain matter.[2] The gate of the chief man, or local magistrate, would here seem to have been the recognized court of justice.

In the palace ruins at Persepolis and Susa, the great doorways show, in their architecture, the influence of Babylonia, Assyria, and Egypt. And in the relief sculpture

---

[1] W. Robertson Smith's *Religion of the Semites,* p. 319.

[2] Strassmaier Nabuchodonosor, No. 183.

of those doorways there is seen a representation of "the king rendering justice at his palace gate."[1]

At one of the gates of modern Cairo, the writer has seen a venerable Arab sitting in judgment on a case submitted to him by the contestants. And such a scene may be often witnessed at the gates of an Oriental city.

In accordance with this primitive idea, it became a custom in India for one who would obtain justice from another to seat himself at the door of a house, or a tent, and refuse to move from that position until he starved to death, unless his claim were heeded. If the suitor died at the door, or the household altar, the sin of his death rested upon the householder. The suitor's blood cried out against the evil-doer.

Even to the present time appeals at the household altar are made in blood, in portions of India. A case recently before the British court in Kathiawar involved an illustration of such an appeal. One of the Charaus, a caste of heralds, had become responsible with his life, according to custom, for repayment of a loan made to a land owner. The land owner delayed payment, and seemed disposed to avoid it. "The herald and his brother, with their old mother for a sacrifice, went to the door of the debtor's house and demanded payment, as their family honor was at stake. When the land owner would not pay, the herald struck off the head of his mother with his sword before the door, the brother at the same time wounded (intending to kill) the debtor, and the two brothers sprinkled the mingled blood of

---

[1] Dieulafoy's L'Art Antique de la Perse;" cited in Babelon's *Manual of Oriental Antiquities*, p.152.

the sacrifice on the householder's door-posts. The land owner, smitten by public infamy and the guilt of the matricide, starved himself to death."[1] References to this responsibility of the heralds are found in the Mahabharata.[2]

Even where the primitive custom of sacrificing at the doorway has died out, there sometimes seems to be a survival of it in popular phraseology. Talcott Williams, of Philadelphia, relates an incident of his experiences in Morocco, which illustrates this. He says: "As I was riding through the Soko at Tangier on a morning in June, 1889, a servant stopped me, and said; 'Four men, from near Azila (a town on the seacoast of Morocco, about thirty miles away), are waiting for you at the gate of the house of Mr. Perdicarus, and they have killed a sheep.' 'What have they killed a sheep for? said I. 'Oh! said the servant, 'I don't mean that they have actually killed a sheep, but they are sitting at the gate, asking for your help, and expect you to aid them in their trouble, because they have heard that you have influence with the American counsul, and are a man of importance in your own country, and we call that "killing a sheep."' I think he added 'at the gate,' but my memory is not perfectly clear at this point. I rode on to the house of my friend, where I was stopping, and found there the kinsman of a sheikh, who had been imprisoned by the American counsul. They seized my horse's bridle, and, with the usual Oriental signs of respect, refused to let me dismount until I had heard them and their plea for help.

---

[1] See *the Times* (London) for July 12, 1894.

[2] See Hopkins' *Religions of India*, p. 361, note.

"I was told by my own servant and the other Orientals there, that this plea 'at the gate,' accompanied as it was by the readiness to 'kill a sheep,' was one which no man in Morocco would dream of disregarding. I made some inquiry on the subject afterwards, and found that the habit of sitting at the gate waiting for a man of supposed influence or authority, while absent, to return to his house, often actually accompanied, though less frequently at present, by the slaughter of a sheep, whose blood is poured across the road over which he must pass, was a form used only in cases of dire necessity, and one to which a man with whom other pleas would avail nothing, felt compelled to give attention. I am glad to add that in my own case this ancient rite was not without its fruits to those who had used it."[1]

See the Bible references to this idea. Moses stood "in the gate of the camp," at a crisis hour in Israel's history, when he would execute judgment in the Lord's cause.[2] All Israel was aroused to do judgment against the sinning Benjamites because of the appeal of the dying woman who fell at the door of the house, "with her hands upon the threshold."[3] Boaz "went up to the gate," to meet the elders there, when he would covenant to do justice by Ruth and the kinsman of Naomi.[4] Absalom sat in "the way of the

---

[1] In a personal letter to the Author.

[2] Exod. 32:26.

[3] Judg. 19:25-30.

[4] Ruth 4:1-10.

gate" when he would show favor to those who came there with their appeals for justice.[1]   And when Absalom was dead, David as king was again sitting in the gate.[2] Zedekiah, the king of Judah, was sitting in the gate of Benjamin when Ebed-melech appealed to him in behalf of Jeremiah.[3]   Daniel's post of honor in Babylon was "in the gate of the king," as a judge in the king's name.[4]

Wisdom, personified, says of him who would seek help where it is to be obtained:

> *"Blessed is the man that heareth me,*
> *Watching daily at my gates.*
> *Waiting at the posts of my doors."*[5]

The Lord's call to Israel, through the prophets, was: "Establish judgment in the gate,"[6] and "Execute the judgment of truth and peace in your gates."[7]   A reference to a just and righteous man is to "him that reproveth in the gate."[8]

---

[1]   2 Sam. 15:2-4.

[2]   2 Sam. 19:8.

[3]   Jer. 38:7-9.

[4]   Dan. 2:4.9.

[5]   Prov. 8:34.

[6]   Amos 5:15

[7]   Zech. 8:16

[8]   Isa. 29:21.

Lazarus in his need is laid daily at the gate of the rich Dives, "seeking help."[1] So, again, the poor man who was a cripple from his birth was "laid daily at the door of the temple . . . called Beautiful, to ask alms of them that entered into the temple."[2]

It is written in the Mosaic law, that, when a bondman would bind himself and his family in permanent servitude to his loved master, "his master shall bring him unto God [or to the place of judgment and of covenant], and shall bring him to the door, or unto the door-post; and his master shall bore his ear through with an awl; and he shall [thenceforward] serve him forever;"[3] or, as it is elsewhere said, the master shall thrust the awl "through his ear, unto [or into] the door."[4] Here, apparently, the master and servant appeal together at the household altar, in witness of their sacred covenant.

The high court of Turkey is still called the "Sublime Porte," the "Exalted Gateway;" and the subjects of the Sultan seek imperial favor at his palace door. He, or his representative, administers justice there, to those who are waiting at his gate.

A promise to Abraham was: "Thy seed shall possess the gate of his enemies."[5] And again Jesus says of his

---

[1] Luke 16:19,20

[2] Acts 3:3,10.

[3] Exod. 21:5,6

[4] Deut. 14:17.

[5] Gen. 22:17.

Church, that "the gates of Hades shall not prevail against it."[1] In both these cases "gates" are obviously equivalent to the power of those who are within the gates. Thus, also, when the overthrow of a city is foretold in prophecy, it is said, that "the gate is smitten with destruction."[2]

7. COVENANT TOKENS ON THE DOORWAY.

Because the threshold of the doorway is the primitive altar of the household, the doorway itself is, as it were, a framework above the altar; and the side-posts are lintel of the doorway fittingly bear tokens or inscriptions in testimony to the sacredness of the passage into the home sanctuary. It would seem that originally the blood poured out in sacrifice on the threshold was made use of for marking the door-posts and lintel with proofs of the covenant entered into between the in-comer and the host; and that afterwards other symbols of life, and appropriate inscriptions, were substituted for the blood itself.

There are survivals in the East, at the present time, of the original method of blood-marking the frame of the doorway; and there are traces of its practice in ancient times in both the East and the West. President Washburn, of Robert College, Constantinople, says:[3] "I remember, after the great fire in Stamboul, in 1865, going over the ruins, and

---

[1] Matt. 16:18.

[2] Isa. 24:12.

[3] In a personal letter to the Author.

coming to a house that the fire had spared; a sheep had been sacrificed on the threshold, and a hand dipped in the blood and struck upon the two door-posts."

This appears, also, in the installing of a Chief Rabbi in modern Jerusalem. In the welcome to the Hakham Bâshi, or the "First in Zion,"[1] "the multitude of those gathered together accompany him to his house, but before he sets the sole of his foot upon the threshold of the outer gate [or court] one of the shokheteem [or official slaughterers] slays a perfect beast, and pronounces the sacrificial blessing, and all those present answer, "Amen." Then the Rabbi, the Hakham Bashi, steps over the beast which has been slain, and the shokhet dips the two palms of his hands into the blood, and marks first the vessels of the rabbi's house. And, with his hands stained with blood, he forms the semblance of a hand above the lintel of the door; —in their trust that this thing is good [the proper thing] for the evil eye; —and the flesh of the beast they distribute to the poor."[2]

A custom in this same line is noted among the Jews in Morocco, in connection with wedding observances. "Wilst the bullock, or other animal, is being slaughtered for the evening's festivities, a number of boys dip their hands in the blood, and make an impression of an outspread hand on the door-posts and walls of the bride's house;" supposedly "for the purpose of keeping off the 'evil eye' and thus ensuring good luck to the newly married couple."[3]

---

[1] See Finn's *Stirring Times*, I., 192f.

[2] A. M. Luncz, in *Jerushalayim*, p. 17.

[3] *Home and Synagogue of the Modern Jew*, p. 30.

There are indications of such a custom in ancient tames. Layard says of his researches in Assyria; "On all the slabs forming entrances in the oldest palaces of Nimroud, were marks of a black fluid resembling blood, which appeared to be daubed on the stone. I have not been able to ascertain the nature of this fluid; but its appearance cannot fail to call to mind the Jewish ceremony of placing the blood of the sacrifice on the lintel of the doorway."[1]

In ancient Egypt there were inscriptions, together with the name of the owner, on the side-posts and lintels of the dwellings. "Besides the owner's name." says Wilkinson,[2] "they sometimes wrote a lucky sentence over the entrance of the house, for a favorable omen, as 'The Good Abode,' the *múnzel mobárak* of the modern Arabs, or something similar; and the lintels and imposts of the doors in the royal mansions were frequently covered with hieroglyphics, containing the ovals and titles of the monarch. It was, perhaps, at the dedication of the house, that these sentences were affixed; and we may infer, from the early mention of this custom among the Jews, that it was derived from Egypt."[3]

When it is understood that the inscribing, on the doorways, of dedications to protecting deities, was common among primitive peoples, it would seem to be in accordance with that custom that the Hebrews were commanded to dedicate their doorways to the one living God. It is said of

[1] *Nineveh and its Remains* (Am.Ed.), II., 202.

[2] Ancient Egyptians, I., 346, 361f.

[3] Comp. Deut. 6:9 and 20:5.

the words of the covenant of God with his people, as recorded in Deuteronomy 6:4-9 and 11:13-21, "Thou shalt write them upon the doorposts of thy house, and upon thy gates." To this day, among stricter Jews, these covenant words inscribed on parchment, and enclosed in a cylinder of glass, or a case of metal or of wood, are affixed to the sideposts of every principal door in the house. This case and inscription are called the "mezuza." On the outside of the written scroll, the divine name, *Shaddai*,—"the Almighty,"—is so inscribed that it may be in sight through an opening in the case or cylinder. This name stands for "the Guardian of the dwellings of Israel," whose protection is thus invoked above the primitive altar of the household on the threshold of the entrance way.[1]

Every pious Jew, as often as he passes the mezuza, touches the divine name with the finger of his right hand, puts it to his mouth and kisses it, saying in Hebrew, 'The Lord shall preserve thy going out and thy coming in, from this time forth, and for evermore:'[2] and when leaving on a business expedition he says, after touching it, 'In thy name, *kuzu bemuchsaz kuzu* (=God), I shall go out and prosper.'"[3] In some cases the covenant words are inscribed directly upon the door-posts, instead of being written on parchment and enclosed in a case.

On the lintels of the ancient synagogues in Palestine there were sculptured symbolic figures, such as the paschal

---

[1] See art, "Mezuza," by Ginsburg, in Kitto's *Cycl. Of Bib. Lit.*

[2] Psa. 121:8.

[3] See art, "Mezuza by Ginsbuerg, in Kitto's *Cycl. Of Bib. Lit.*

lamb, a pot of manna, a vine, or a bunch of grapes, together with inscriptions; and the doorposts were ornamental more or less richly.[1] Evidences of this are still abundant.

Speaking of the writing over the door and all round the room at the office of the consul in Sidon, Dr. Thomson says that Muhammadans "never set up a gate, cover a fountain, build a bridge, or erect a house, without writing on it choice sentences from the Koran, or from their best poets. Christians also do the same."[2] These writings are deemed a protection against harm from evil spirits.

In Persia, both the Muhammadans and the Armenians inscribe passages from their sacred books above their doorways, with ornamental adornings, in "strange, fantastic patterns."[3] The palace doorways in ancient Persia were inscribed and ornamented in a high degree.[4]

At the present time, in China, coins are put under the door-sill at the time of its laying, and charms are fastened above the door;[5] the gods of the threshold are invoked at the doorway by shrines and inscriptions, while sentences, as in ancient Egypt, are written on the side-posts and lintel.[6] At

---

[1] See, for example, *Memoirs of Survey of Western Palestine*, I., 230-234, 257f. 309-402, 407f., 416f.

[2] *The Land and the Book*, I., 140f.

[3] See Sir Robert Ker Porter's *Travels*, I., 440.

[4] See, for example, Perrot and Chipiez's *Hist. Of Art in Persia*, pp. 127, 129, 294, 357; also, Benjamin's *Persia and the Persians,* pp. 17, 52, 61.

[5] Doolittle's *Social Life of the Chinese*, II., 75, 310f.

[6] William's *Middle Kingdom*, I. 731.

the festival of the fifth month of the Chinese year, "charms, consisting of yellow paper of various sizes, on which are printed images of idols, or of animals, or Chinese characters, are pasted upon the doors and door-posts of houses, in order to expel evil spirits." In times of pestilence, sentences written in human blood are fastened on the door-posts for protection from disease.[1]

Describing a ceremony on a large Chinese junk when starting out on a long voyage, an observer tells of the sacrifice of a fowl in honor of the divinity called Loong-moo, or the Dragon's Mother. A temporary altar was erected at the bow of the vessel, as its beginning, or threshold, and the blood of the sacrificed fowl was shed there. Pieces of silver paper were "sprinkled with the blood [of the fowl], and then fastened to the door-posts and lintels of the cabin."[2] The cabin door is the home door of the voyager.

Above the house door of almost every home, in large portions of Japan, there is suspended the shimenawa, or a thin rope of rice straw, which is one of the sacred symbols of ancient Shintoism. Above the doors of high Shinto officials, this symbol is of great size and prominence. Its presence is as a sign of a covenant with the gods.[3]

The Greeks certainly recognized the entrance of the house as the place for an altar to the protecting deity.

---

[1] Adele M. Fielde's *Pagoda Shadows*, p. 88.

[2] Gray's *China*, II., 271. Comp. with p. 3.

[3] Hearn's *Glimpses of Unfamiliar Japan*, II., 397; also, Isabella Bird's *Unbeaten Tracks in Japan*, II., 287.

"Before each house stood, usually, its own peculiar altar of Apollo Agyieus, or an obelisk rudely representing the god himself;" and that over the house door, "for good luck," or as a talisman, "an inscription was often placed."[1] And on occasions, as when a bride entered her husband's house, the doorway was "ornamented with festive garlands."[2] Theocritus refers to a Greek custom of smearing the side-posts of the gateway with the juice of magic herbs, as a method of appeal to the guardian deity to influence the heart of the dweller within toward the suppliant at the door.[3]

Roman householders affixed to the lintels and side-posts of their doors the spoils and trophies taken by them in battle. Branches, and wreaths of bay and laurel, were hung by them in the doorway on a marriage occasion; and lamps and torches were displayed at their doors at other times of rejoicing; while cypresses were shown there at the time of a death.[4]

Texts of Scripture, and other inscriptions, as a means of invoking a blessing at the doorway, are frequently found at the present time above the entrance of houses in South Germany.

In Central America and in South America the blood of sacrificial offerings was smeared on the doorways of houses

---

[1] See Becker's *Charicles*, p. 260, with citations; also, Guhl and Koner's *Life of the Greeks and Romans,* p. 80.

[2] Becker's *Charicles*, p. 487.

[3] Theocritus, *Idyl* II., 63.

[4] See articles "ara" and "Janua," in Smith's *Dict. of Greek and Roman Antiquities,* with reference to classical authorities.

as well as of temples, as a means of covenanting with the local deities. Illustrations of this are found in the records and remains of Peru[1] and Guatemala.[2]

In both Europe and America, the practice of nailing horseshoes on the side-posts of a doorway, for "good-luck," or as a means of guarding the inmates of the house from evil, is very common. So lately as the seventeenth century is was said: "Most houses of the West End of London have the horseshoe on the threshold."[3] Even at the threshold of Christian churches, in recent years, the symbol of the horseshoe was to be found as a means of protection. [4] The horseshoe is often to be found on a ship's mast. At the present time, horseshoes of various sizes, for use as doorway guards against evil, are found on sale in Philadelphia, and other centers of civilization.

8. SYMBOL OF THE RED HAND.

It would seem that, in primitive practice, the hand of the covenanter dipped in the sacrificial blood on the threshold, and stamped on the door-posts and lintel, was the sign-manual of the covenant between the contracting party or parties, and God, or the gods invoked in the sacrifice.

---

[1] See Reville's *Native Religions of Mexico and Peru, p.* 183.

[2] See Rowan in "Ximenes," p. 183; cited in Spencer's *Des.Soc.* ,II. ,22.

[3] Aubrey's "Miscellanies;" cited in *Gentleman's Magazine* for 1823, Pt. II., p. 412.

[4] See *Gentleman's Magazine* for 1867, Pt.I., pp.307-322.

Illustrations of this custom, as still surviving in the East, have been given, from Constantinople, Jerusalem, and Morocco.[1] Naturally, therefore, the sign-manual by itself came to stand for, or to symbolize, the covenant of the threshold altar; and the stamp of the red hand became a token of trust in God or the gods covenanted with in sacrifice, and of power or might resulting from this covenant relation. Wherever the red hand was shown, or found, it was a symbol of covenant favor with Deity, and it came to be known, accordingly, as the "hand of might."

In the region of ancient Babylonia, also, the red-hand stamp is still to be seen on houses and on animals, apparently as the symbol of their covenant consecration by their owner. Dr. Hilpreacht says: "Over all the doors of the rooms in the large khan of Hillah, on the Euphrates, partly built upon the ruins of ancient Babylon, I noticed the red impression of an outspread hand, when I was there in January, 1889. Several white horses in our caravan from Bagdad to Nippur had the stamp of a red hand on their haunches."

This symbol is much used in Jerusalem. Referring to its frequency, Major Conder says: "The 'hand of might' is another Jewish belief which may be supposed to have an Aryan origin. This hand is drawn on the lintel or above the arch of the door. Sometimes it is carved in relief, and before one house in the Jews' quarter, in Jerusalem, there is an elaborate specimen, carefully sculptured and colored with vermilion. Small glass charms, in the form of the hand, are also worn, and the symbol is supposed to bring

---

[1] See p. 62f., supra.

good luck. The Jewish and Arab masons paint the same mark on houses in course of construction; and, next to the seven-branched candlestick, it is probably the common house-mark in Jerusalem."[1]

A Jerusalem Jew thus tells of its use among a portion of his co-religionists in that city: "Our brethren the Sephardeem [the Spanish Jews], like all the remnant of the sons of the East, consider the semblance of a hand as good against the power of the evil eye in a man. And they draw this shape upon the doors of their houses with a red finger. So, too, they place upon the heads of their children a hand wrought in silver, saying that this hand—or this picture of the five fingers—is noxious to the man who delights to bring the evil upon the child, or upon those dwelling in the house. So, again, when men quarrel, the one sets his five fingers before the other's evil eye, saying that this sign neutralizes the evil."[2]

This sign of the hand is "found on the houses of Jews, Muslims, and Christians, in various parts of Palestine." It is generally painted on or above the door, often in blue; but frequently, especially when a Jew or a Muhammadan enters a new house, a lamb is sacrificed at the door, and the stamp of the hand in the fresh blood is affixed to the doorpost or to the walls.[3] No one claims to know the origin of this symbol, but all recognize its importance.

In its ruder form the figure of the hand is much like a

---

[1] *Heth and Moab*, p. 275,f.

[2] A. M. Lunez, in *Jerushalayim*, p. 19.

[3] On the testimony of the Rev. W. Ewing, a missionary in Palestine.

five-branched candlestick. Indeed, it has sometimes been mistaken for that symbol. This was the case when such a figure was noticed, not long ago, by Dr. Noetling, on Jewish houses in Safed, and reported to a European journal. This symbol is sometimes called the "Hand of Moses." A similar figure on Muslim houses is said to represent the "Hand of the Prophet;" while in Syria, among Christians, it is called the *Kef Miryam*, the "Virgin Mary's Hand."[1] Obviously these terms suggest the idea of power through divinely derived strength.

One of the sights in the Mosk of St. Sophia, in Constantinople, is the stamp of a red hand. It is said that when Sultan Muhammad II, entered this sanctuary as a conqueror, he dipped his right hand in the blood of the slaughtered Christians, and stamped it on the wall, as if to seal his victory, and to pledge his covenant devotion to his God.[2] Whether this story be fact or legend, it is a witness to the idea of such a custom in the minds of Oriental peoples.

An open hand is, or was, a common symbol on a banner, as also on a prayer-rug, in both Turkey[3] and Persia. At the annual festival in Persia in commemoration of the death of Hossein, son of Alee, two large banners, each surmounted with an open hand, are borne in front of the representation of the tomb of Hussein; and the same symbol

---

[1] In *Zeitschrift Des Deutschen Palestina Vereins,* VIII., 335ff.

[2] See De Admicis's *Constantinople*, p. 185

[3] One of these old-time prayer-rugs with the open hand embroidered on it, is in the possession of Dr. Hilprecht.

appears in various ways during the celebration.[1]

"In the East Indies, to this day, the figure of a hand is the emblem of power and governmental sway. When the Nabob of Arcot was the viceroy of five provinces, if he appeared in public there were carried before him certain little banners, each with a hand painted on it, and a larger banner with five hands."[2]

Siva, the destroyer, in the Hindoo triad, is also the re-creator; since death is only the entrance into a new life. One of Siva's well-known symbols is a hand, which is a token of might and life.

The uplifted open hand was prominent on or above the doors in ancient Carthage.[3] And a traveler in Northern Africa, writing of the Jews in Tunis, near the site of Carthage, says: "What struck me most in all the houses was the impression of an open bleeding hand on every wall of each floor. However white the walls, this repulsive sign was to be seen everywhere. A Jewess never goes out here without taking with her a hand carved in coral or ivory - she thinks it a talisman against the 'evil eye,' or *'mal occhio'* . . . When his children's pictures or horses are praised, the Tunisian Jew extends his five fingers, or pronounces the number 'five;' he tries by this means to prevent the praise doing damage."[4]

---

[1] See Morier's *Second Journey Through Persia, pp.* 75-184.

[2] Rosenmuller's *Das Alte Und Neue Morgenland*, II.,92f.

[3] See, for example, Perrot and Chipiez's *History of Art in Phoenicia*, I., 54, 263.

[4] De Hesse-Warteg's *Tunis: the Land and the People*, p. 127.

This symbol of an open hand is frequently found above the graves in the vicinity of Tunis. It is also seen in old Jewish cemeteries in Europe, as, for instance, in Prague.[1]

An open hand, in stone, or metal, or enamel, or bone, used as a talisman or an amulet, to guard the wearer against evil, was in common use in ancient Egypt. Specimens of these can be seen in museums in Europe and America today.

It is a noteworthy fact that the uplifted hand is prominent in the representation of the deities of Babylonia, Assyria, Phoenicia, and Egypt, especially of the gods of life, or of fertility, who have covenant relations with men. And the same is true of the representations of sovereigns, in the ancient East, who are supposed to be in peculiar covenant relations with the gods.

Thus, on the seal of Ur-Gur, the earliest ruler of "Ur of the Chaldees,"[2] the ruler and his attendants appear with uplifted hands before the moon-god Sin, who in turn is represented with his hand uplifted, as if he were making covenant with them.[3] It is the same with the sun-god Shamash and his worshipers.[4]

When a king of ancient Babylon was recognized as having a right to the throne, he must lift up his hand and clasp the hand of the image of Bel-Merodach, in order to

---

[1] On the testimony of Professor Dr. Morris Jastrow, Jr.

[2] Gen. 11:31; 15:7.

[3] Perrot and Chipiez's *Hist of Art in Chald. And Assy.*, I., 38; see, also, p. 84.

[4] *Ibid.*, I.,203.

show that he had "become the adopted son of the true ruler of the city." This giving and taking of the hand was a symbol of covenanting in Babylonia. In this way a child was adopted into a family and a husband and a wife covenanted to become one.[1]

The god Asshur, and his worshipers, kings or princes, are similarly represented in Assyria with the hand uplifted. And it is the same there with other deities and their worshipers.[2] In Phoenicia, and its colonies, the same idea has prominence.[3]

Deities of ancient Egypt are frequently represented with the uplifted hand, and their accepted worshipers appear before them with the right hand uplifted.[4] As showing that this is not the attitude of supplication or of adoration, like the bowed form, the crossed arms, or the upturned palms, it is to be noted that in the representation of Amenophis IV., or Khuen-aten, with his family, before the aten-ra or the solar disk, the worshipers stand with their right hands uplifted, while the sun-god reaches down a series of open hands, as if in covenant proffer to the uplifted hands below.[5]

[1] Sayce's *Social Life among the Assyrians and Babylonians*, p. 52f.

[2] Perrot and Chipiez's *Hist. Of Art in Chald. And Assy.*, I.,p.196. See also, pp. 87, 143, 212; II., 99, 111, 169, 211, 215, 227, 231, 257, 261, 266, 267, 273, 275, 279. See, also, *Collection De Clercq. passim*.

[3] Perrot and Chipiez's *Hist. Of Art in Phoenicia*, I., 53, 54, 69 ,320; II., 61, 113, 161, 223, 247, 248, 255, 257.

[4] Wilkinson's *Anc. Egypt*, III., 3, 8, 24, 48, 53, 100, 192, 208, 218, 228, 232, 235, 240, 362, 370, 425.

[5] *Ibid.*, III., 53.

In the county of Roscommon, in Ireland, there is a stone known as "a druidical altar," which the common people say was thrown there by the giant Finmac-Coole, "the print of whose five fingers, they say, is to be seen on it." The hand-print is pointed to confidently as the proof of authenticity, as if it were the veritable signature of the giant.[1]

Among the ruins in Central America, there were found at the doorways and on the walls of many of the ruined buildings of Yucatan the stamp of a red hand on the plaster or on the stone. "They were the prints of a red hand, with the thumb and fingers extended, not drawn or painted, but stamped by the living hand, the pressure of the palm upon the stone. He who made it had stood before it alive, . . . and pressed his hand, moistened with red paint, hard against the stone. The seams and creases of the palm were clear and distinct in the impression." As showing the idea prevalent among the natives of that region with reference to the source and meaning of these signs-manual, the Indians of Yucatan said that the stamp was of "the hand of the owner of the building," as if he had affixed it to his dwelling in token of his covenant with its guardian deity; and, again, it was thought that "these impressions were placed there in a formal act of consecration to the gods."[2]

There is a clear recognition of this idea in many Bible references to the lifting up of the hands unto God, as if in covenant relations with him. Thus, Abraham says to the

---

[1] Mason's *Statistical Account* or *Parochial Survey of Ireland*, II., 322.

[2] Stephens' *Incidents of Travel in Yucatan*, I., 177f.

king of Sodom, "*I have lift up my hand unto the Lord;*"[1] as if he would say, I have pledged myself to him. I have given him my hand. And the Psalmist says: "*I will lift up my hands in thy name.*"[2] God himself says, by his prophet: "*I will lift up mine hand to the nations;*"[3] that is, I will covenant with them."[4] And so in many another case. Indeed, the Assyrian word for swearing (*Nish*) is literally "lifting up the hand;"[5] and the Hebrew word *nasa* means to lift up the hand or to swear.[6] The uplifted hand in a judicial oath seems to be a survival of the same thought, that an appeal is thus made to God, as one's covenant God.

Again, there may be a reference to the "hand of might" in a covenant relation, in those passages where God is spoken of as bringing his people out of Egypt by "*a strong hand,*" or "*a mighty hand,*" and as dealing with them afterwards in the same way.[7]

An uplifted hand is a symbol found also on the stepped

---

[1] Gen. 14:22.

[2] Psa. 63:4.

[3] Isa. 49:22.

[4] Comp. Exod. 6:8; Num. 14:30; Neh. 9:15.

[5] See Tallquist's *Die Sprache Contracte Nabu-naido*, p. 108.

[6] See Gesenius's *Heb. Lex.*, s. v. "Nasa."

[7] See, for example, Exod. 3:19; 13:3,14,16; 32:11; Deut. 3:24; 4:34; 5:15; 6:21; 7:8, 19; 9:26; 11:2, etc; 2 Chron. 6:32; Ezek. 20:34; Dan. 9:15.

pyramid temples of Polynesia.[1]

This sign of the red hand is still a familiar one among the aborigines of America. It is stamped on robes and skins, and on Indian tent.[2] Schoolcraft says of it: "The figure of the human hand is used by the North American Indians to denote supplication to the Deity or Great Spirit, and it stands in the system of picture-writing as the symbol for strength, power, or mastery, thus derived (through a covenant relation). In a great number of instances which I have met with of its being employed, both in the ceremonial of their dances and in their pictorial records, I do not recollect a single one in which this sacred character is not assigned to it."[3]

A frequent use of the hand-print among the American Indians is as "a symbol applied to the naked body after its preparation and decoration for sacred and festive dances." These preparations are "generally made in the arcanum of the medicine, or secret lodge, or some private place, and with all the skill of the priest's, the medicine-man's, or the juggler's art. The mode of applying it in these cases is by smearing the hand of the operator with white or colored clay, and impressing it on the breast, the shoulder, or other part of the body. The idea is thus conveyed that a secret influence, a charm, a mystic power, is given to the dancer, arising from his sanctity, or his proficiency in the occult arts." Schoolcraft, speaking of this custom, says: "The use

---

[1] Ellis' *Polynesian Researches*, II., 207, illustration.

[2] Stephens' *Incidents of Travels in Yucatan*, II., 46f.

[3] Stephens' *Incidents of Travel in Yucatan*, Appendix, II., 476-478.

of the hand is not confined to a single tribe or people. I have noticed it alike among the Dacotah, the Winneabagoes, and other Western tribes, as among the numerous branches of the red tribes, as among the numerous branches of the red race still located east of the Mississippi River, above the latitude of 42 degrees, who speak dialects of the Algonquin language."[1]

Is there possibly any connection with this idea in the custom of "the laying on of hands," as a symbol of imparting virtue or power to one newly in covenant relations with those who are God's representatives, so frequently referred to in the Bible?[2] This would seem to be indicated by the power imparted to an Egyptian king by the touch of the uplifted hand of the deity, as shown in the representations on the monuments of Egypt. It was known as "the imposition of the Sa," or increased vitality.[3]

A remarkable illustration of the use of the red-hand print among American Indians is given in the story of a famous Omaha chief, who, when dying, enjoined it upon his followers to carry his body to a prominent look-out bluff above the Missouri River, and bury him there, full armed, on the back of his favorite horse, who was to be buried alive, that he might watch from that place the passing of the

---

[1] *Ibid.*, II.,477.

[2] See Gen. 49:8-17; Num. 27:22f; Acts 4:4; 6:6; 8:18; 13:3; 19:6; Heb. 6:2; I Tim. 4:14.

[3] See, for example, "a scene in the hypostyle hall at Luxor," in Maspero's *Dawn of Civilization, p.* 111; also, illustration in Perrot and Chipiez's *Hist. Of Art in Anc. Egypt,* I.,45.

whites up and down the river. It would seem as if he wanted to be known as dying in the faith of his covenant relations with the Great Spirit, for himself and for his people.

Because of this request, in the presence of his assembled tribe "he was placed astride his horse's back, with his bow in his hand, and his shield and quiver slung; with his pipe and his medicine bag; with his supply of dried meat, and his tobacco pouch replenished; . . . with his flint and steel, and his tinder, to light his pipe by the way. The scalps that he had taken . . . were hung to the bridle of his horse. He was in full dress and equipped; and on his head waved . . . his beautiful head-dress of the war-eagle's plumes." As he stood thus on the threshold of the life beyond, when the last funeral honors were performed by the medicine men, "every warrior of his band painted the palm and fingers of his right hand with vermilion, which was stamped and perfectly impressed on the milk-white sides of his devoted horse," —as if in covenant pledge of fidelity to their chief in the sight of the Great Spirit.[1]

There is another phase of the red-hand symbolism among the American Indians, which has been noted by Frank H. Cushing, who is so experienced and careful an observer of their customs and ceremonies. This phase connects the symbol directly with the idea of life and its transmission. Mr. Cushing says:[2]

---

[1] Catlin's Eight Years amongst the North American Indians," II., pp. 5-7; cited in Donaldson's *George Catlin Indian Gallery*, p. 263.

[2] In a personal letter to the Author.

"By reference to the paintings (and writings, to some extent) of such men as Catlin and Stanley, and to the works of Schoolcraft, Matthews, Bourke, and others, you will find that the red-hand symbol was painted on the lodges, sometimes on the clothing and person, and sometimes on the shields of various of the hunter tribes of the plains, —as, for example, of the Ioways, Sauks and Foxes, Sioux Arickarees, Cheyennes, Arapahoes, and Comanches. Precisely what the significance of the symbol was, with these peoples and others like them, I am not able to say, save that in some cases it was connected with war, in others with treaties, and in yet others as expressive of power. There were yet other meanings attached to the sign, but neither the former significances nor these latter were, I take it, as definite or fixed (with the hunter tribes) as with the more advanced and settled tribes of the farther south.

"Of these tribes, the typical Pueblos and the peoples more or less directly influenced by them—such as the Jicarillas on the north and east, and the Apaches to the south and west[1]—made frequent use of not only the red-hand symbol, but also of the black-hand symbol. I have seen both, not only in the modern but also in the very ancient pueblos—as those of the Pecos, and those of the great cliff-dweller towns in the Chelly and other canyons. In the Pecos ruins, to give a special example, I copied beautiful hand-paintings and prints from the rafters, as well as from the walls of ordinary dwelling-rooms. Sometimes these

---

[1] See Bourke's *Medicine Men of the Apaches*, Ninth Annual Report of the Bureau of Ethnology.

paintings were in red, but more often in black. They invariably represented the hands of women, as could be seen by their delicacy and smallness of outline and by their shapeliness. There was, I think, a reason for this, which the following facts will explain.

"It was my good fortune to witness, early in the eighties, a ceremonial celebrating the attainment to puberty, or womanhood, of a young girl of the Jicarilla Apaches. The latter people are not to be confounded with the Apaches proper. They are a mixed people, descended not only from the Apaches, but also the Comanches, and in large part also from the Pueblos of the north, the so-called Tanoans of whom the Pecos people were a branch. It was clear from the character of the masks and other paraphernalia used in the ceremonials I witnessed, that the latter were almost, if not quite, wholly derived from the pueblo, rather than from the wilder, ancestry of the Jicarillas who performed them.

"The ceremonial in question was performed by four medicine-men, or priests, as one might call them, within and around a rectangular enclosure of evergreen boughs set in the plain near to the village. Inside of this enclosure, which was designed to screen from view the more secret operations of the priest dancers in question, stood a little conical skin lodge, the snow-white top of which the young girl, over whom these rites were being enacted, was ensconced, together with one or two old women of the tribe. As I have said before, each of the priests, on appearing (and this they did successively; that is, the first on the first day, the second on the second day, and so on), wore a conical mask or helmet, which entirely concealed, not only the face, but also the head. This mask was painted black or red, and upon the face of it appeared one of these hand symbols. Unfortunately, I did not see the mask as worn by the first priest, but as worn by the second priest on the morning of the second day, it bore upon its face the symbol of the red hand, and as worn upon the third day, this symbol recurred, but, if I remember aright, was surrounded by an outline of another color, either black or yellow, whilst the hand painted on the mask as worn on the fourth day was black surrounded by white, that it might stand out more conspicuously; and in turn, below it, were two or more dots alternating with dotted circles.

"My means of communicating with these people were but limited, but on learning that the ceremonials they were performing were designed to celebrate the attainment to maturity, or womanhood, of a virgin, I had little difficulty in understanding the significance of the succession of these various hand symbols. I recognized in the ceremonial as a whole the dramatic epitomization, to state it briefly, of the four ages of a woman's life. Thus the white hand (which I was told had been painted on the mask of the first day) symbolized her infancy and girlhood, the consummation of which was effected by the first day's ceremonial performed by the medicine-man of the white hand.

The red-hand was obviously significant of this girl's attainment to young womanhood, the color in this case symbolizing the blood of her perfected life. I imagine that the black hand painted on the mask as worn during the third day's ceremonial was significant of not only the betrothal of the girl, which was said to have taken place during that day of the ceremonial, but also of her prospective maternity; the change of color, in the hand, from red to black, being naturally a symbolic representation of the change from red to black in blood that has been exposed to the sunlight and dried, and has thus become black, and is no longer virgin. Likewise the hand painted on the mask as worn during the fourth day's ceremonial, which was wholly black, doubtless represented the fuller life of not only a matron but a grandmother. From this I would infer that the signs of the red and black hands found in the ruined pueblos like those of Pecos, and on the cliffs at the mouths of caves, or in the houses of the cliff villages, symbolized respectively virginity, and maternity or betrothal.

"What would seem to indicate the correctness of this conclusion is the fact that, as I have mentioned before, there were below the signs of the black hand of the last day's ceremonial of the Jicarillas dots and dotted circles. It is well known that these dots and dotted circles represent, primarily, grains of corn, male and female; and, secondarily, children, male and female. Their occurrence, then, below the painted black hand or symbol of maternity, would indicate that in this case they represented the children and perhaps grandchildren, male and female, of the matron it was hoped this young girl might become.

"The hand symbol as occurring amongst the Zuñi, with whom, of course, I am much more familiar, has not only some such significance of a given symbol depending upon the ceremonial with which it is associated, and particularly upon the coloring which is given to it, the colors being as various as are the well-known seven sacramental colors employed to symbolize the seven regions of the world by the priesthood of these people.

"I will only add, that the hand-symbol painted upon the

walls of the estufas, or Kiva temples, or upon the little sacred sand mounds, which are made to symbolize mythic mountains of the six regions during the ceremonials of initiation performed once every four years over the new children of the pueblo, are designed to signify the various ritualistic percepts which are taught to the children according as they are held to pertain to one or another of these little sand mounds or so-called mountains of generation.

"In the case above described I was told, although I did not myself see it, that the symbol of the red hand was painted by the side of the entrance to the little tent in which the girl sat through the ceremonials, and that later the same symbol in black was added to the other side of the entrance to this tent. In the case of the Pueblos the position of the hand symbols depends, as, no doubt, you have already inferred, upon the sort of ceremonial which is being performed in connection with them.

"It would seem, however, that the placing of these symbols at the *entrance* of the cave villages would correspond to such usages as I have above described as pertaining to the Jicarilla ceremonial, and that the painting of them on the rafters of rooms in ancient pueblos had a like connection; for it must be remembered that in the older pueblos there were no doorways proper [hence no thresholds]. The rooms were entered by means of ladders through scuttles in the roof."[1]

A hand-print is a signature. A hand-print in blood is a pledge of life in a sacred covenant. A hand-print in the blood of life is symbolic of a covenant of life with a view to the transmission of life. When a woman of Korea is married, she affixes her sign manual to the covenanting contract by placing her hand on the paper and having "the outline drawn round the fingers and wrist with a fine brush dipped in Chinese ink," or again she employs "the simpler process of smearing her hand with black paint, and hitting the document with it.[2]

Formal documents have often been signed by a hand stamp, or a finger stamp, in blood or in ink. The monks of the convent of St. Catherine at Mt. Sinai, for instance, show a copy of the certificate of protection given to them by the Prophet of Islam, the signature to which is an impression of Muhammad's open hand. A letter to Muhammad Issoof, from the king of Mysore, in 1754, was sealed with the king's seal, "and on the back was stamped the print of a hand, a form equivalent, with the Mysoreans, to an oath."[3]

The very term "sign manual," employed for a veritable

---

[1] For illustrations of this truth see II. Ploss's *Das Weib in der Naiur, und Volkerkunde* (ad ed.), I., Chap.39; Strack's *Der Illutaberglaube* (4th ed.), pp. 14-18; Spivak's *Menstruatikon*, pp.6-12; and Frazer's *Golden Bough*, I., 170; II., 225-240. These illustrations are gathered from Asia, Africa, Europe, America, and the Islands of the Sea; and they include citations from Pliny, the Talmud, the Christian Fathers, medieval writers, and down to writers of this century.

[2] Landor's *Corea* or *Cho-sen*, p. 156.

[3] Orme's *Hist. Of Milit. Trans. Of British in Indostan*, V., 348.

signature, may point to an origin in this custom. Indeed, may it not be that the large red seal attached to important documents, at the present time, is a survival of the signature and seal of the bloody hand?

9. DEITIES OF THE DOORWAY.

Originally the covenant sacrifice at the threshold was with the one God of life. But as monotheism degenerated into polytheism, the idea came to prevail of different deities in different portions of the door, or of different deities in different districts of country or in different offices of life.

Each gate of an Assyrian city was dedicated to a special god, and named after it,—as the gate of Bel, the gate of Beltis, the gate of Anu, the gate of Ishtar. At the entrance-way of every gate gigantic winged bulls with human heads stood on guard, accompanied by winged genii.[1] And the central doorway to the king's palace was similarly guarded.[2] In every house a special deity was appealed to at different portions of the doorway; Nergal on the top of the wall and beneath the threshold; Ea and Merodach in the passage to the right and left of the gate.[3]

The idea of an offering, or of a dedication, to the local divinity, at the time the threshold is laid, is of wide acceptance. In India, "the god Vāttu, or Vātuma [a son of

---

[1] Maspero's *Life in Anc. Egypt and Assyria, pp.* 198-220.

[2] *Ibid.* p. 204.

[3] *Ibid.,* p .220.

Vishnoo], is said to recline and live in the threshold, changing his position every month . . . On the day when the door-frame and threshold of a new house or temple are fixed, the *Vāttuyma santhe* (the tribute to Vāttuma) is offered.[1]

In China, "Shintu and Yuhlui are named as two tutelar gods to whom the guardianship of the house is entrusted; and either the names or grotesque representations of these 'gods of the threshold' are at the gate of the house, with shrines to them upon the left of the entrance way."[2]

It is said of these "Chinese gods of the threshold," that "in full stature, and presumably in primeval strength, they flank the doors of monasteries and the entrances to the halls of justice. Much reduced in size and perched high on shelves, they face each other in the vestibules of the Chinese home; and in their most diminutive aspect they become little images, occasionally two-headed, which are carried about the person as charms, or hang from the eaves of Chinese houses."[3]

Over the doors of almost all the houses of Japan are to be seen small prints of the "gigantic *Ni-o*, the Booddist Gog and Magog," who are supposed to guard the entrance way of the holy places.[4] Private buildings as well as public need

---

[1] Robert's *Oriental Illustrations of the Scriptures*, p. 148f.

[2] William's *Middle Kingdom*, I., 731.

[3] See McDowell's "A New Light on the Chinese," in *Harper's Magazine for* Dec., 1893, with illustrations of "The Gods of the Threshold."

[4] Isabella Bird's *Unbeaten Tracks in Japan*, I., 117, 273.

this spiritual protection.

The inscriptions at the doorways of the houses of ancient Egypt showed that every building was "placed under the protection of a tutelary deity." This custom "is retained by the modern Egyptians in the protecting genius said to preside over the different quarters of Cairo."[1]

Tertullian, a Christian Father who wrote before the close of the second century, in warning believers against the seducements of idolatry, emphasized the clustering of deities at the doors and gates in the religions of Greece and Rome.[2] He says that "among the Greeks . . . we read of Apollo Thyraeus (that is, of the door), and the Antelii (or, Anthelii) demons, as presiders over entrances," Cardea (Hinge-goddess), called after hinges; and Forculus (Door-god) after doors; and Limentinus (Threshold-god) after the threshold; and Janus (Gate-god) himself after the gate."

Although a Christian might not recognize these gods as gods, he is told to beware lest he seem to give them honor by adorning his gates with lamps or wreaths. "Indeed, a Christian will not even dishonor his own gate with laurel crowns," says Tertullian, "if so be he knows how many gods the devil has attached to doors." And his words of warning are: "Since there are beings who are adored in entrances [doorways], it is to them that both the lamps and laurels will pertain. To an idol you will have done whatever you shall

---

[1] Wilkinson's *Manners and Customs of the Ancient Egyptians,* I., 362f., and note.

[2] See Tertullian "On Idolatry," and "On the Soldier's Chaplet," in *Ante-Nicene Christian Library,* XI., 164f., 353.

have done to an entrance [or doorway]." "If you have renounced [heathen] temples, make not your own gate a [heathen] temple." Yet, in proof of the prevalence of this heathen custom among Christians, Tertullian testifies: "'Let your works shine,' says He; but now all our shops and gates shine! You will now-a-days find more doors of heathens without lamps and laurel-wreaths than of Christians."

In Guatemala, in Central America, "the god of houses" is called Chahalka; and the blood of sacrifices to him is sprinkled on the door of the houses as an assurance of his protection.[1]

It was much the same in the Old World as in the New. In ancient and in modern times, and in widely different portions of the world, there are indications that the threshold of the home was the primitive altar; and that the side-posts and lintel of the door-way above the threshold bore symbols or inscriptions in proof of the sacredness of the entrance to the family home, and in token of an accomplished covenant with its guardian God, or gods.

[1] Tr. Rowan, in Ximenes," p. 183; cited in Spencer's *Descrip. Soc.*, I., 22.

II.

EARLIEST TEMPLE ALTAR.

I. FROM HOUSE TO TEMPLE.

A temple is only a more prominent house. As a house was the dwelling of the earlier priest of his household, who was in covenant for himself and his family with the guardian deity of that household; so, afterwards, a temple was a dwelling for the deity guarding an aggregation of families, and for the priests who stood between him and the community.

This is no new or strange truth; it is obvious, "In the Vedas, Yama, as the first man, is the first priest too; he brought worship here below as well as life, and 'first he stretched out the thread of sacrifice.'"[1] The fire-altar of the home was the first center of worship in the family in India;[2] as later the fire-altar was the center of the worship of the community.

The same cuneiform characters in old Babylonian stand

---

[1] Darmesteter's translation of *Zend Avesta*, in *"Sacred Books of the East."* IV., 12, note.

[2] De Coulange's *Ancient City*, pp. 32-35, 46f.

for great house, for palace, and for temple;[1] as similarly, in ancient Egypt, the same hieroglyph represented house or temple,—a simple quadrangular enclosure, with its one doorway.[2]

The oldest form of an Egyptian temple known to us through the inscriptions of the Ancient Empire indicates that the prehistoric houses of worship in that land were mere hovels of wood and lattice-work, over the doors of which was a barbaric ornamentation of bent pieces of wood.[3] The private house became the public temple.

"The design of the Greek temple in its highest perfection was . . . a gradual development of the dwelling-house."[4] Palace and temple were, indeed, often identical in ancient Greece.[5]

Strictly speaking, there were no temples in ancient Persia, any more than in early India. But the fire-altars that were first on the home hearth, or threshold, were made more and more prominent on their uplifted stepped bases, until they towered loftily in the sight of their worshipers.

It is the same Hebrew word, *ohel*, that stands for the "tent" of Abraham, and for the "Tent" or Tabernacle of the

---

[1] Compare Friedrich Delitzsch's *Assyrisches Handwörterbuch*, s. v. "Ekalla."

[2] Wilkinson's *Egyptians in the Times of the Pharoahs*, p. 141.

[3] Erman's *Life in Ancient Egypt*, p .279f.

[4] Guhl and Koner's *Life of the Greeks and Romans*, p. 297

[5] See, for example, *Odyssey*, VII., 80.

congregation of Israel.[1]

In China "temple architecture differs little from that of the houses."[2] The house of a god is as the house of a man, only grander and more richly ornamented. And Japanese antiquaries say that the architecture of Shinto temples is on the model of the primeval Japanese hut. The temples of Ise, the most sacred of the Shinto sanctuaries, are said to represent this primitive architecture in its purest form [3]

The father of the family was the primitive priest in the Samoan Islands, and his house was the first place of worship. Then "the great house of the village," or the place of popular assembling, was used as a temple; and afterwards there were special temple structures with attendant priests.[4]

The transition from house to temple seems to have been a gradual one in the primitive world. The fire-altar of the family came to be the fire-altar of the community of families. The house of a king became both palace and temple, and so again the house of a priest; for the offices of king and of priest were in early times claimed by the same person.[5]

---

[1] Comp. Gen. 18:1-9, and Exod. 26:1-14; 39:32, etc.

[2] Douglas's *Society in China, p* .343

[3] See Chamberlain's *Things Japanese*, pp. 37, 226f, 378; Griffis's *Mikado's Empire*, p. 90; Isabella Bird's *Unbeaten Tracks in Japan*, II., 282.

[4] Turner's *Samoa*, pp. 18-20.

[5] Maspero's Dawn *of Civilization*, p. 703f.

2. SACREDNESS OF THE DOOR.

In all stages of the transition from house to temple, the sacredness of the threshold, of the door, of the entrance-way, of the gate, was recognized in architecture and in ceremonial. Often the door, or the gate, stood for the temple, and frequently the threshold was an altar, or an altar was at the threshold.

There are, indeed, reasons for supposing that the very earliest form of a primitive temple, or sanctuary, or place of worship, was a rude doorway, as covering or as localizing the threshold altar. This would seem to be indicated by prehistoric remains in different parts of the world, as well as in the later development of the idea in the earlier historic ages. The only exception to this was where, as in India or Persia, the fire-altar on an uplifted threshold stood alone as a place of worship.

Two upright stone posts, with or without an overlaying stone across them, and with or without an altar stone between them, are among the most ancient remains of primitive man's handiwork; and a similar design is to be recognized, all the way along in the course of history, down to the elaborate doorway standing by itself as a memorial of the revered dead,[1] or to the monumental triumphal arch as an accompaniment of the highest civilization. And the very name of door, or gate, attaches persistently to the loftiest temple and to the most exalted personage. As the earliest altar was the threshold, the earliest temple was a doorway

---

[1] See Fergusson's *Rude Stone Monuments*, pp. 100, 411-413.

above the altar at the threshold.

When the first dweller on the plains of Chaldea, after the Deluge, gathered themselves for the building of a common structure reaching God-ward,[1] they, in their phraseology, called that structure Bab-el, or Bâb-ilu, or Bâbi-ilu, the Door of God,[2] Ancient Egyptians called the sovereign head of their national family *"Per-ao"* (Pharaoh), the exalted House, or Gate, or Door;[3] as today the Sultan, who is spiritual father of the faithful Muhammadans, and autocrat of his realm, is widely known as the "Sublime Porte," or the Exalted Door.[4] The modern Babists, in Persia and beyond, look up to their spiritual head as the "Bab," or the "Door."[5] "Throughout the East this word ['Bab'] signifies the court of a prince [as a ruler by divine right] . . . The threshold of the gate is used in the same sense, and frequently it is qualified by some epithet of nobility, loftiness, or goodness."[6]

---

[1] Gen. 11:1-9

[2] See Mihlau and Vole's Gesenius's *Heb. Und Aram, Handworterbuch* (12th ed.), s. v. "Babel;": also Schrader in Richon's *Dict. Of Bib. Antiq.* (2nd ed.).

[3] See Brugsch's *Egypt under the Pharoahs*, I., 63; also Erman's *Life in Ancient Egypt,* p. 58.

[4] See Perrot and Chipiez's *History of Art in Chal. And Assy.*, II., 72.

[5] See Count de Gobineau's *Les Religions et Les Philosophies dans l'Asia Centrale'* also Browne's *Year among the Persians*, and Traveller's *Narrative to Illustrate the Episode of the Bab.*

[6] *Bibliotheque Orientale*, s.v., "Bab."

Jesus Christ did not hesitate to say of himself as the Way to God; *"I am the Door: by me if any man enter in he shall be saved."*[1]

In China, Japan, Korea, Siam, and India, a gate, or doorway, usually stands before Confucian and Boodhist and Shinto temples, but apart from the temple, and always recognized as of peculiar sacredness. These doorways, in many places, are painted blood-color. [2] They stand "at the entrance of temple grounds, in front of shrines and sacred trees, and in every place associated with the native *"kami"*—or gods. [3] Yet again, in all these countries, the temple gateway is a main feature, or a prominent one, in the chief sanctuaries. [4]

Swinging doors, or gates, are represented, in the religious symbolism of ancient Babylonia, as opening to permit the god Shamash, or the sun, to start out on his daily circuit of the heavens.[5] A door, or a doorway, appears as a shrine for a god in various cylinders from this region; and the god

---

[1] John 10:9.

[2] See, for example, Griffis's *Mikado's Empire*, p. 419; Isabella Bird's *Unbeaten Tracks in Japan*, I, 295f; II., 367f, Gray's *China*, I., 99; Fergusson's *Rude Stone Monuments*, p. 413.

[3] See Chamberlain's *Things Japanese*, p. 429f; and, Lowell's *Choson*, pp. 262-266, for a fuller explanation of the origin and signification of this primitive entrance way.

[4] See, for example, Douglas's *Society in China*, p .411; Isabella Bird's *Unbeaten Tracks in Japan*, I., 64; Fergusson's *Tree and Serpent Worship*, frontispiece, plates iv-ix, xxi.

[5] See Maspero's *Dawn of Civilization*, p. 656.

is shown standing within it, just beyond the threshold.[1]
Indeed, the doorway shrine is a common form on the
Babylonian and the Assyrian monuments, as a
standing-place for the gods, and for the kings as
representative of the gods.[2] Illustrations of this are found on
the Balawat gates,[3] and the sculptures on the rocks at
Nahr-el-Kelb[4]—which is itself a gateway of the nations,
between the mountains and the sea, on the route between
Egypt and Canaan, and both the East and the West.

In ancient Egypt the doorway shrine of the gods was
prominent, as in Babylonia.[5] Moreover, a false door was
represented in the earlier mastabahs, or tombs, of the Old
Empire of Egypt. This representation of a door was toward
the west, in which direction Osiris, the god of the
under-world, was supposed to enter his realm as the sun
went down. On or around this false door were memorial
inscriptions and prayers for the dead; and before it was a

---

[1] *Ibid*, p. 569. The doorway in the engraving from the intaglio is clearly
one of the doorway shrines, with the guardians of the doorway on either side,
and not, as has been supposed, an opening into the ark.

[2] Maspero's *Dawn of Civilization*, pp .657, 662, 759, 762; also Perrot and
Chipiez's *Hist. Of Art in Chal. And Assy..*, I., 203, 212; II. 95, 163, 210,
211.

[3] *Ibid.*,II., facing p. 212.

[4] Perrot and Chiqiez's *Hist. Of Art in Chal. And Assy.*, II., 231; Perrot and
Chipiez's *Hist. Of Art in Phoenicia and Cyprus*, I., 9. See also, note in
Rawlinson's *Herodotus*, II., pp. 148-151.

[5] Wilkinson's *Anc. Egypt*, III., 349; Erman's *Life in Anc. Egypt*, pp. 274,
283; and Maspero's *Dawn of Civilization*, pp.189-239.

table, or altar, for offerings to the *ka*, or soul, of the dead.[1] Gradually this false door came to be recognized as the monumental slab, tablet, or stele, on which were inscribed the memorials of the deceased. As a doorway or a niche, square-topped, or arched, it was the shrine of the one worshipped; and as a panel, or independent stele, it was the place of record of the object of reverence.

"Even at the beginning of the Middle Empire the door form disappeared completely, and the whole space of the stone was taken up with the representation of the deceased sitting before a table of offerings, receiving gifts from his relatives and servants. Soon afterwards it became the custom to round off the stone at the top, and when, under the New Empire, pictures of a purely-religious character took the place of the former representations, no one looking at the tomb stele could have guessed that it originated from the false door."[2]

A "false door" was, in ancient Egypt, a valued gift from a sovereign to an honored subject. Doors of this kind were sometimes richly carved and painted, and were deemed of priceless value by the recipient.[3]

---

[1] Erman's *Life in Anc. Egypt*, p. 311; Maspero's *Dawn of Civilization*, pp. 237, 250, 253, 262, 316, 413.

[2] Erman's *Life in Anc. Egypt*, p. 314. See, also illustrations in Perrot and Chipiez's *Hist. Of Art, in Anc. Egypt*, I., 131, 140, 175.

[3] Erman's *Life in Anc. Egypt*, p. 319.

In Phoenicia,[1] Carthage,[2] Cyprus,[3] Sardinia,[4] Sicily,[5] and in Abyssinia,[6] a like prominence was given to the door as a door, in temple and in tomb, and as a niche for the figure of a deity or for the representation of one who had crossed the threshold of the new life. And the door-form is a sacred memorial of the dead in primitive lands in various parts of the world, from the rudest trilithon to the more finished structures of a high civilization."[7]

In primitive New Zealand the gateway, or doorway, of a village, a cemetery, or a public building, is both a sacred image and a sacred passage-way. It is in the form of a superhuman personage, and it has its guardians on either hand.[8]

A doorway with an altar between its posts was a symbol of religious worship in ancient Mexico, as in the far East.[9]

---

[1] Perrot and Chipiez's *Hist. Of Art in Phoenicia and Cyprus*, I., 256; II., 31, 57, 147, 178.

[2] *Ibid.*, I., 53, 54.

[3] *Ibid.*, I., 287; II., 147.

[4] *Ibid.*, I., 264, 321.

[5] *Ibid.*, I., 320.

[6] Bent's *Sacred City of the Ethiopians*, pp. 185-193.

[7] See, for example, Fergusson's *Rude Stone Monuments*, pp. 109, 168f., 217, 233, 335, 337, 385, 388, 398-401, 411-413, 441, 464, 468, 484, 532.

[8] See illustrations in Sherrin's *Early History of New Zealand*, pp. 406, 514, 648.

[9] Bancroft's *Native Races*, IV., 481.

It would seem that the "mihrab," or prayer niche, pointing toward Meccah, in Muhammadan lands, and the Chinese honorary portals and ancestral tablets,[1] as well as the niches for images of saints in churches or at wayside shrines, or for heroes in public halls, in Christian lands, are a survival of the primitive door-way in a tomb.

And wherever the door is prominent as a door, the threshold is recognized and honored as the floor of the door, and as the primitive altar above which the door is erected. To pass through the door is to cross over the threshold of the door.

3. TEMPLE THRESHOLDS IN ASIA.

In all the modern excavations in the region of Babylonia and Assyria, including Tello, Nippur, Sippara, Borsippa, Khorsabad and Nineveh, it has been found that the threshold, or foundation stone of the temple doorway is marked with inscriptions that show its peculiar sanctity; while underneath it, or near it, are frequently buried images and symbols and other treasures in evidence of its altar-like sacredness. On this point evidence has been furnished by

---

[1]   See, for example, Williams' *Middle Kingdom*, I., frontispiece; Gray's *China*, I., 11f.

Botta,[1] Bonomi,[2] Layard,[3] George Smith,[4] Lenormant,[5] and yet more fully by Dr. Hilprecht, in his later and current researches.

Bonomi suggests that the word "teraphim," as an image of a household divinity, has its connection with the threshold or the boundary limit; and that the phrase "thy going out, and thy coming in," which is common in Egyptian, Babylonian, and Hebrew[6] literature, has reference to the threshold and its protecting deities.[7] The outgoing and the incoming are clearly across the threshold and through the door.

The inscriptions of Nebuchadnezzar II, concerning his building of the walls of Babylon, comprise various references to the foundations, to the thresholds, and to their guardians. He says: "On the thresholds of the gates I set up mighty bulls of bronze, and mighty snakes standing

---

[1] See citation in Bonomi's *Nineveh and its Palaces* (2d ed.), pp. 157-160, 174.

[2] *Ibid.*

[3] *Nineveh and its Remains* (Am.ed.), II., 202.

[4] *Assyrian Discoveries*, pp. 75, 78, 429.

[5] *Chaldean Magic*, pp. 47, 48, 54.

[6] See, for example, I Sam. 29:6; 2 Sam. 3:25; 2 Kings 10:27; Psa. 121:7,8; Isa. 37:28; Ezek. 43:11.

[7] See references to the Mezuza of the Hebrews at page 63f., supra.

upright."[1] Again of the gates of Imgur-Bêl and Nimitti-Bel, of these walls of Babylon, he says: "Their foundations I laid at the surface (down at) the water, with pitch and bricks. With blue enameled tiles which were adorned with bulls and large snakes, I built their interior cleverly. Strong cedars I laid over them as their covering (or roof). Doors of cedarwood with a covering of copper, a threshold (*askuppu*) and hinges of bronze, and powerful snakes standing upright, I set upon (or at) their threshold (*sippu*). Those gates I filled with splendor for the astonishment of all mankind."[2]

In a similar manner Nebuchadnezzar describes his work at the gates of "the royal castle of all mankind," at Babylon,[3] and of his palace.[4] In connection with the shrine or chapel of Nebo(Ezida), within the walls of the temple of Merodach, in Babylon, he says: "Its threshold (*sippu*), its lock and its key, I plated with gold, and made the temple shine daylike."[5] When he built Ezida (the "eternal house"), the temple of Borsippa, Nebuchadrezzar says: "The bulls and the doors of the gate of the sanctuary, the threshold (*sippu*), the lock, the hinge, I plated with Zarîru"[6] (an

---

[1] Grotefend Cylinder, Col. I., 11. 44-46. See, also, Rawlinson's *Cuneiform Inscriptions of Western Asia.*, Vol.I., p. 65, Col. I., II. 19-21.

[2] *East India House Inscription*, Col. III., II, 48-50.

[3] *Ibid.*, Col. VIII., II, 5-9.

[4] *Ibid.*, Col, IX., II , 9-16.

[5] Grotefend Cylinder, Col. I., II. 36-38.

[6] *East India House Inscr.*, Col. II., II. 48-50.

unknown metal, a kind of bronze).

References to the foundations, to the thresholds, to the gates and doorways, and to bulls and upright serpents, as the guardians of the threshold of the temples and palaces of Babylonia and Assyria, are numerous on unearthed cylinders and tablets, and always in such a way as to indicate their peculiar sacredness. In the recent unearthing, at Nippur, of a small building or shrine, between two great temples, an altar was found in the eastern doorway.

It is to be borne in mind that many early temples in Babylonia, as in Mesopotania, in Egypt, in Mexico, Central America, and Peru, and in the South Sea Islands, were in the form of a stepped pyramid, or a staged tower, with either inclined planes or stairways from each lower stage to the next higher, and with an altar, or a sanctuary or shrine, at the summit.[1] Herodotus, describing one of these temples in Babylon, says that the altars, larger and smaller, were outside the temple.[2]

Light is thrown on the dream of Jacob at Bethel by the shape of the ancient temple in the East. In his vision it was probably not a ladder, but a conventional stepped-temple structure, with its stairways rising heavenward, and its

---

[1] See Layard's *Nineveh and Babylon* (Am.ed.), p. 424; Perrot and Chipiez's *Hist. Of Art in Chald. And Assy.*, I., 366-392; Rawlinson's *Herodotus*, Bk.II. ,Chap.99, 125; Sayce's *Religion of the Ancient Babylonians*, p. 96; Mariette Bey's *Monuments of Upper Egypt*, p. 79f.; Bunsen's *Egypt's Place in Universal History*, II., 378-386; Rawlinson's *History of Ancient Egypt*, I., 188-194; Reville's *Religions of Mexico and Peru*, pp. 41f., 179f.; Ellis' *Polynesian Researches*, II., 207.

[2] Rawlinson's *Herodotus*, Bk, I., Chap. 181-183.

sanctuary, that Jacob saw.[1]   The angel ministers were passing up and down the steps, in the service of the Most High God, who himself appeared above the structure. When Jacob waked, he said: *"Surely the Lord is in this place [or sanctuary]; and I knew it not . . . How dreadful is this place! This is none other but the house of God, and this is the gate of heaven;"* and he took the stone which had been his pillow at the threshold of that sanctuary, and set it up for an altar pillar.[2]

In the literature and legends of Babylonia, as of other portions of the ancient world, there is prominent the idea that an entrance into the life beyond this, as in the entrance into this life, the crossing of a threshold from one world to the other, from the earlier state and the passing of a door, or gate, marks the change to the later, from the sacred to the more sacred. This is peculiarly illustrated in the famous legend of Ishtar's descent into the under-world in order to bring back to earth her lover Dumuzi.

The Hades of the Babylonians was surrounded by seven high walls, and was approached through seven gates, each of which was guarded by a pitiless warder. Two deities ruled within it—Nergal, "the lord of the great city," and Beltis-Allat, "the lady of the great land,"—whither everything which had breathed in this world descended after death. Allat was the actual sovereign of the country; and

---

[1]   The word "sullam," here translated "ladder," is a derivative from "salal," "to raise up in a pile, to exalt by heaping up as in the construction of a mound or highway." Comp. Isa. 57:14; 62:10; Jer. 50:26, See Bush's *Notes on Genesis*, in loco.

[2]   Gen. 28:10-22.

even the gods themselves could enter her realm only on the condition of submitting to death, like mortals, and of humbly avowing themselves her slaves.[1] "The *threshold* of Allat's palace stood upon a spring, which had the property of restoring to life all who bathed in it or drank of its waters." Yet it was needful that another life should be given for one who would be reborn into this life, after crossing the threshold of the regions beyond.[2]

In the descent of the goddess Ishtar into Allat's realm, in pursuit of her lover Dumuzi, Ishtar was gradually stripped of her garments and adornings at the successive gates, until she appeared naked, as at birth, at the final threshold of the new state.[3] But she was held captive by Allat until Ea, chief among the gods, exerted himself in her behalf, and sent his messenger to secure for both Ishtar and Dumuzi the waters of life which were underneath the threshold of Allat's realm,—which must be broken in order to their outflowing.[4]

There would seem to be a reference to this primitive idea of the waters of life flowing from under the threshold of the temple, in the vision of the prophet Ezekiel, writing in Babylonia, concerning restored Jerusalem and its holy temple. "*Behold, waters issued out from under the threshold of the house eastward, for the forefront of the house*

---

[1] See Maspero's *Dawn of Civilization*, pp .691-696, with citation of authorities at foot of p. 693, and note at p. 695.

[2] *Ibid.*; also Sayce's *Relig. Of the Anc. Babyl.*, pp. 221-278; 286, note 3.

[3] Comp. Job 1:21; Eccl. 5:15; I Tim. 6:7.

[4] Maspero's *Dawn of Civilization*, p. 696.

was toward the east; and the waters came down from under, from the right side of the house, on the south of the altar." (Evidently the altar in this temple was near the threshold.) These flowing waters from under the threshold were life-giving. *"Upon the bank of the river,"* as it swelled in its progress, *"were very many trees on the one side and on the other;"* and it was said of this stream: *"It shall come to pass, that every living creature which swarmeth, in every place whither the rivers come, shall live; and there shall be a very great multitude of fish; for these waters are come thither, . . . and everything shall live whitersoever the river cometh."*[1] In a curse pronounced against Assyria by the prophet Zephaniah, it was declared that "drought shall be in the thresholds,"[2] instead of life-giving waters.

So, again, the waters of the life-giving Jordan flow out from the threshold of the grotto of Pan, a god of life.[3] And both at the beginning of the Old Testament, and at the close of the New, the waters of life start from the sanctuary of the Author of life.[4]

This Dumuzi of Babylonia has linkings with Tammuz of Syria, with Osiris of Egypt, and with Adonis of Greece, and there are correspondences in all these legends in the references to the door and the threshold of the under-world and the life beyond. Thus, for instance, the Lord's prophet

---

[1] Ezek. 47:1-9.

[2] Zeph. 2:13,14, with margin.

[3] See *Survey of Western Palestine*, 'Memoirs,' I.,107.

[4] See Gen. 2:8-10; Rev. 22:1,2.

counts as most heinous of all idolatries the transfer of the weeping worship of Tammuz from the door in the hole of the temple wall to the door of the temple sanctuary.[1]

At the right hand of the entrance of the larger temple unearthed at Nineveh by Layard, a sculptured image of the Assyrian king, with his arm uplifted, was on a doorway stele just outside. And an altar for offerings was in front of that image. Altars were found similarly situated, just outside the doorway, in a smaller temple in the same region.[2]

An exceptional reverence is shown to the doorway and threshold of their sanctuary, or temple, by the sect of the Yezidis, in the neighborhood of ancient Nineveh, at the present time. Describing an evening service which he attended, Layard says: "When the prayers were ended, those who marched in procession kissed, as they passed by, the right side of the doorway leading into the temple, where a serpent is figured on the wall." Again, "Soon after sunrise, on the following morning, the sheikhs and cawals offered up a short prayer in the court of the temple . . . Some prayed in the sanctuary, frequently kissing the threshold and holy places within the building."[3]

When the sacred ark of the Hebrews was captured by the Philistines, and brought into the house of the god Dagon, the record is: *When they of Ashdod arose early on the morrow, behold, Dagon was fallen upon his face to the ground before the ark of the Lord. And they took Dagon,*

---

[1] Ezek. 8:8-16.

[2] Layard's *Nineveh and Babylon* (Am.ed.), pp. 302-311.

[3] *Ibid.*, p. 69f.

and set him in his place again. And when they arose early on the morrow morning, behold, Dagon was fallen upon his face to the ground before the ark of the Lord; and the head of Dagon and both the palms of his hands lay cut off upon the threshold." It is added, in our present Bible text: "*Therefore neither the priests of Dagon, nor any that come into Dagon's house, tread on the threshold of Dagon in Ashdod, unto this day.*"[1]

It would seem, from the words "unto this day," that this added statement was a gloss by a later writer or copyist. The original force of the wonder was in Dagon's being overthrown at his very shrine, falling maimed on the threshold altar of his temple. But the suggestion of the gloss is that the unwillingness of the Philistines to tread on the threshold of the temple (which appears to have been of primitive origin) did not exist among the worshipers of Dagon prior to this incident. The Septuagint adds,[2] concerning the later practice of the Philistines at the threshold, "because leaping they leap over it."

Leaping over the threshold is at times spoken of in the Bible as if it had a taint of idolatry. Thus Zephaniah, foretelling, in the name of the Lord, the divine judgments on idolaters, says: "*In that day I will punish all those that leap over the threshold.*"[3] This is explained in the Targum as "those that walk in the customs of the Philistines." Yet the Bible sometimes refers to the temple threshold as a fitting

---

[1]   I Sam. 5:1-5.

[2]   In Loco.

[3]   Zeph. 1:9.

place of worship, and its recognition as a holy altar as commendable.

Ezekiel prophesies that the restored Prince of Israel "*shall worship at the threshold of the gate*"[1] of the Lord's house; and he sees, in vision, "*the glory of the Lord . . . over the threshold of the house.*"[2] Again the Lord complains of the profanation of his temple by idolaters "*in their setting of their threshold by my threshold, and their door-post beside my door-post, and there was but the wall between me and them*"[3]

That it was the threshold or doorway of the tabernacle which was counted sacred, is evident from the wording of the Levitical laws concerning the offering of blood in sacrifices. "*This is the thing which the Lord hath commanded, saying, What man soever there be of the house of Israel, that killeth an ox, or lamb, or goat, in the camp, or that killeth it without the camp, and hath not brought it **unto the door of the tent of meeting,** to offer it as an oblation unto the Lord before the tabernacle of the Lord; blood shall be imputed unto that man; he hath shed blood; and that man shall be cut off from among his people: to the end that the children of Israel may bring their sacrifices, which they sacrifice in the open field, even that they may bring them unto the Lord, **unto the door of the tent of meeting,** unto the priest, and sacrifice them for sacrifices of peace offerings unto the Lord. And the priest shall sprinkle the*

---

[1] Ezek. 40:2.

[2] *Ibid.* 10:4; 9:3.

[3] *Ibid.* 43:8.

blood; **upon the altar of the Lord at the door of the tent of meeting,** *and burn the fat for a sweet savour unto the Lord . . . Whatsoever man there be of the house of Israel, or of the strangers that sojourn among them, that offereth a burnt offering or sacrifice, and bringeth it not* **unto the door of the tent of meeting,** *to sacrifice it unto the Lord; even that man shall be cut off from his people.*"[1]

It was **at the doorway** of the tent of meeting that Aaron and his sons were consecrated to the holy priesthood;[2] and it was there that the bullock was sacrificed, and its blood was poured out as an offering at the base of the altar.[3] It was **at the doorway** of that tent, above the threshold, that the pillar of cloud descended in token of the Lord's presence, when Moses met the Lord there in loving communion, while the people stood watching from the doorways of their own tents.[4] The altar of burnt offering, at the base or foundation of which the blood of the offerings was outpoured, was itself at the doorway of the tent of meeting, and he who offered a sacrifice to the Lord offered it at that threshold.[5]

A post of honor in the temple was as a guardian of the threshold, as was also the place of a keeper of the gate. In

---

[1] Lev. 17:2-9

[2] Exod. 29:4.

[3] *Ibid.*, 29:10-12

[4] Exod. 33:8-10; see, also, Num. 12:5; 20:6; Deut. 31:15.

[5] See, for example, Exod. 40:6,29; Lev.I:3,5; 3:2; 4:4,7; 8:1-36; 12:6; 14:11, 23; 15:14, 29; 16:7; 17:4-9; 19:21; Num. 6:10-18.

the assignment of the priests and Levites to service, by Jehoiada the priest, in the days of Athaliah, a third part of them were in attendance at the "threshold," and a third part *"at the gate of the foundation."*[1] Later, in the days of Josiah and Hilkiah, the guardians of the threshold had the care of the money collected for the repairs of the Lord's house.[2] And a keeper of the threshold, or of the door, of the house of God, was always mentioned with honor.[3] When the Psalmist contrasts the house of God with the tents of wickedness, he speaks of the honor of a post at the temple threshold, not of the humble place of a temple janitor, when he says:

"For a day in thy courts is better than a thousand [else-where]. I had rather stand at the threshold of the house of my God, Than to dwell in the tents of wickedness."[4]

In the Temple at Jerusalem, the altar of burnt offering was before the threshold of the Holy Place; and those who came with sacrifices must stop at that threshold, and proffer the blood of their offering to the priests, who then reverently poured it out at the altar-threshold's base.[5]

---

[1] 2 Chron. 23:4,5.

[2] *Ibid.*, 34:8,9.

[3] I Chron. 15:23,24; Jer. 35:4; 52:24, etc.

[4] Psa. 84:10.

[5] See Edersheim's *The Temple: Its Ministry and Services*, p. 191; also, Ginsburg's art, "Passover," in Kitto's *Cycl. Of Bib. Lit.*, p. 420.

When offerings were accepted for the repairs of the temple, in the days of Jehoash, king of Judah, it is said that *"Jehoiada the priest took a chest, and bored a hole in the lid of it, and set it beside the altar, on the right side as one cometh into the house of the Lord. And the priests that kept [or guarded] the threshold put therein all the money that was brought into the house of the Lord."*[1] This would seem to decide the position of the altar as at the threshold, where *"one cometh into the house of the Lord."*

An altar stood at the doorway, or before the door, of temples of later date in Phenicia and Phrygia, as shown on contemporary medals and coins.[2] And so in temples in other lands.

Among the early Christian remains unearthed in Asia Minor are indications of the former position of an altar on the threshold of a sanctuary. At the site of ancient Aphrodisias, "some of the sarcophagi of the Byzantine age are richly wrought, and although many are of Christian date, they appear to have retained the pagan devices." At the end of one of these sarcophagi "appears an altar burning in front of a door," standing indeed on the very threshold.[3]

An oath of peculiar sacredness among Hindoos is at the threshold of a temple, as at its primal altar. "Is a man accused of a great crime? He goes to the temple [threshold], makes his prostrations; he pauses, then steps over it,

---

[1] See 2 Kings 12:9; 22:4; 25:18.

[2] See, for example, representation and description of temples at Byblus and Baalbee, in Donaldson's *Architectura Numismatica*, pp. 105f., 122-128.

[3] Fellows's *Travels and Researches in Asia Minor*, p. 256.

declaring at the same time that he is not guilty of the crime laid to his charge. It is therefore very common to ask a person who denies anything that he is suspected to have done, 'Will you step over the threshold of the temple?'"[1]

Among the stories told in India of judgments at the temple threshold, is one of a thieving goldsmith, who had secreted himself in a pagoda of Vishnoo, in order to take from the sacred image one of its jewel eyes. Having obtained the precious stone, he waited for the opening of the pagoda doors in the morning, in order to escape with his booty. But as he attempted to cross the threshold, when the door was opened, he was stricken with death by Vishnoo "at the very threshold."[2] Justice was administered at the very seat of justice.

Bloody sacrifices are still known at the temple thresholds in India, notwithstanding the prejudice of Hindoos against the shedding of blood. Within recent times an English gentleman, in an official position in India, discovered a decapitated child at the very door of a celebrated pagoda; and an investigation showed that a father had there sacrificed his son to avert an impending evil.[3]

When a famous idol was destroyed in the temple of Somnauth, during the Muhammadan conquest of India, pieces of the shattered image were sent by the conquerors to the mosks of Meccah, Medina, and Ghuznee, to be thrown

---

[1] Roberts' *Oriental Illus. Of Scrip.*, p. 143f.

[2] Maurice's *Indian Antiquities*, V., 89.

[3] Maurice's *Indian Antiquities*, V.,7 9f., note. Compare Trumbull's *Blood Covenant*, pp. 157-164.

down at the thresholds of their gates, there to be trodden under foot by devout and zealous Mussulmans.[1] The accursed idol fragments might be trampled on at the threshold, even while the threshold itself was counted sacred.

In Muhammadan mosks generally the threshold is counted sacred. Across the threshold proper, at the beginning of the sacred portion of the interior, "is a low barrier, a few inches high."[2] Before this barrier the worshiper stops, removes his shoes, and steps over it, with the right foot first. In some smaller mosks a rod above the outer door-sill stands for this barrier.

Describing his visit to one of the mosks in Persia, Morier says: "Here we remarked the veneration of the Persians for the threshold of a holy place . . . Before they ventured to cross it, they knelt down and kissed it, whilst they were very careful not to touch it with their feet."[3]

On the tomb of the kings of Persia, at Com, the inscription appears: "Happy and glorious the believing one who in reverence bows his head upon the threshold of this gate, in imitation of the sun and moon.[4] All that *he* will ask with faith in this gate, shall be as the arrow that reaches the

---

[1] Maurice's *Modern Hist. Of Hindostan*, Pt.I., Bk.2, Chap.3, p.296f.

[2] Hughes' *Dictionary of Islam*, art. "Masjid;" also Conder's *Heth and Moab*, p. 293f.; also Lane's *The Modern Egyptians*, I., 105.

[3] Morier's *Second Journey Through Persia*, p. 254.

[4] The moon is said to have thus bowed before Muhammed, at the threshold of the Kaabeh at Meccah. *Anecdotes Arabes et Mussulmans*, p. 22f. (By J. F. de la Croix, Paris, 1772.)

mark."[1] And on the tomb of Alee, son-in-law of Muhammad and one of his successors, there stands the declaration: "The angel messenger of the truth, Gabriel, kisses every day the threshold of thy gate; for that is the only way by which one can come to the throne of Muhammad."[2]

Even among Christians in the primitive region, this reverence for the threshold as the earliest altar of the temple and the church manifests itself in various ways. Mr. Grant, an American missionary, tells of seeing the Nestorian Christians kissing the threshold of the church on entering the sanctuary for the Lord's Day service.[3]

At Baveddeen, near Bokhara, is the tomb of Bahaed-deen Nakishbend, the national saint of Turkestan, which is a place of pilgrimage second only to the tomb of Muhammad. "In the front of the tomb," as a threshold, is the famous *senghi murad*, the "stone of desire," which has been tolerably ground away, and made smooth by the numerous foreheads of pious pilgrims that have been rubbed upon it."[4]

A peculiar sacrifice in Tibet is the disemboweling of a devotee in the presence of a great multitude, as an act of worship. An altar on which this act is performed is erected for the occasion "in front of the temple gate."[5]

---

[1] Chardin's *Voyage*, I.,282.

[2] *Ibid.*, I., 292.

[3] Laurie's *Dr. Grant and the Mountain Nestorians*, p. 134f.

[4] Vambery's *Travels in Central Asia*, p. 233.

[5] Hue's *Travels in Tartary, Thibet, and China*, I., 191.

In the more sacred shrines of Japan and Korea, Shinto or Booddhist temples, pilgrim worshipers are permitted to go no farther than the threshold of the inner sanctuary. There they may deposit their offerings and may prostrate themselves in prayer, but they cannot pass beyond.

At Kitzuki, "the most ancient shrine of Japan," multitudes of pilgrims gather for worship. They are coming and going ceaselessly, but all pause before the threshold of the inner sanctuary. "None enter there: all stand before the dragon-swarming door-way, and cast their offerings into the money-chest placed before the threshold; many making contributions of small coin, the very poorest throwing only a handful of rice into the box. Then they clap their hands, and bow their heads before the threshold, and reverently gaze through the hall of prayer at the loftier edifice, the holy of holies beyond it. Each pilgrim remains but a little while, and claps his hands but four times; yet so many are coming and going that the sound of the clapping is like the sound of a cataract."[1] The same is true of "the great Shrines of Ise, chief Mecca of the Shinto faith,"[2] of those of famous Nikkō, and of other centers of worship.[3]

---

[1] Hearn's *Glimpses of Unfamiliar Japan*, I., **188.**

[2] Lowell's *Occult Japan*, pp. 270-273; also, Isabella Bird's *Unbeaten Tracks in Japan*, II., 278-285.

[3] *Ibid.*, I., 111-119; II., 286-288.

4. TEMPLE THRESHOLDS IN AFRICA.

The oldest temple discovered in Egypt is little more than a doorway with an altar at its threshold, and with a stele on either side of the altar. This temple is near the base of the stepped pyramid of Meydoom, dating back probably to the beginning of the fourth dynasty.[1]

Later, in Egypt, as in early Babylonia, the door-way, above the threshold, had peculiar sacredness, in the temples and in the approaches to the under-world. The pylon, or propylon, of an Egyptian temple, was a monumental gateway before the temple, and exalted honor attached to it. It frequently gave its name to the entire temple.[2] The side towers of this gateway are said to have represented Isis and Nephthys, and the door itself between these towers stood for Osiris, the judge of the living and the dead.[3]

There was indeed a temple in Thebes which bore the name of "Silver Threshold." This temple "is mentioned in the time of the twenty-first dynasty; and it cannot have been earlier than the eighteenth dynasty, when silver was

---

[1] See Petrie's *Ten Years' Digging in Egypt*, pp. 138-142; also, Mariette's *Monuments of Upper Egypt*, p. 107f., and Maspero's *Dawn of Civilization*, pp. 358-361.

[2] Brugsch's *Egypt under the Pharaohs*, I., 67.

[3] See Wilkinson's *Manners and Customs of the Ancient Egyptians*, I., xiv.

growing cheaper in Egypt."[1] But the prominence of the "threshold" in the designation of the "temple" is aside from the question of the time of the use of silver.

"The winged sun disk was placed above all the doors into the temples, that the image of Horus might drive away all unclean spirits from the sacred building."[2] These over-shadowing wings marked the special sacredness of the doors beneath them.

When an Egyptian priest opened the door of the shrine—the holy of holies of the temple—he must prostrate himself at the threshold in reverent worship. "According to the Theban rite, . . . as soon as he saw the image of the god he had to 'kiss the ground, throw himself on his face, throw himself entirely on his face, kiss the ground with his face turned downward, offer incense,' and then greet the god with a short petition"[3] This priestly worship was at the threshold of the shrine.

The Egyptian idea of the future life, and of the world beyond this, had marked correspondences with the Babylonian. Osiris presided over the under-world, as, indeed, he was the chief object of worship in this.[4] He had been slain

---

[1] This is on the testimony of Prof. W. Max Miller, who adds that "so far the Egyptologists have not paid any attention to the threshold;" hence there is a lack of material yet available as showing its peculiar sacredness.

[2] Erman's *Life in Anc. Egypt*, p. 272.

[3] Lemm's "Ritual Book," p. 29ff., 47; cited in Erman's *Life in Anc. Egypt*, p. 274f.

[4] Erman's *Life in Anc. Egypt*, pp. 260, 308f.; Mariette Bey's *Monuments of Upper Egypt, p.* 26.

in a conflict with evil, and in his new life he was the friend
and helper of those who struggled against evil.[1] He was in
a peculiar sense the door of the life beyond this, "Osiris,
opening the ways of the two worlds;"[2] and those who
passed that door safely were identified with himself in the
under-world.[3]

A closed door toward the west, in a tomb, represented
the deceased on his way to Osiris.[4] And as shown in the
"Book of the Dead" the approach to Osiris was by a series
of doors, which could be passed only by one who showed
his identification with Osiris, and his worthiness as such.[5]
At the entrance to the Hall of the Two Truths, or of the
Two-fold Maāt,[6] as the place of final judgment, the deceased was challenged by the threshold of the door, by the
two side-posts, by the lock, by the key, and by the door
itself; and he could not pass these unless he proved his
oneness with Osiris by his knowledge of their names severally.[7]

A saint's tomb, called a *wely,* is a common place of
worship in Egypt. Sometimes a mosk is built over it and

---

[1] Wilkinson's *Ancient Egyptians*, III, 65-80.

[2] *Book of the Dead*, CXI, II.

[3] Renouf's *Relig. Of Anc. Egypt*, p. 191f.

[4] See p. 106, supra.

[5] *Book of the Dead*, CXLV.,CXLVI.

[6] Renouf's *Religion of Ancient Egypt*, p. 202f.

[7] *Book of the Dead*, CXXV.

sometimes it serves as a substitute for a mosk, where no mosk is near. "At least one such building forms a conspicuous object close by, or within almost every Arab village;" and these tombs are frequently visited by those who would make supplication for themselves, or intercession for others, or who would do a worthy act, and merit a correspondent blessing. "Many a visitor, on entering the tomb, kisses the threshold, or touches it with his right hand, which he then kisses."[1] Similar customs prevail in Arabia and Syria.

At Carthage, which was a Phenician colony but which impressed its character on northern Africa, the chief temple gave prominence to the threshold, rising in steps as an altar before a statue of the Queen of Heaven. Virgil, describing the arrival of Aeneas at the court of Queen Dido, says:

> "There stood a grove within the city's midst,
> Delicious for its shade; where when they came
> First to this place, by waves and tempest tossed,
> The Carthaginians from the earth dug up
> An omen royal Juno had foretold
> That they should find, a noble horse's head;
> Thus intimating that this race would shine,
> Famous in war, and furnished with supplies
> For ages. Here the great Sidonian queen
> A temple built to Juno, rich in gifts,
> And in the presence of the goddess blessed,
> A brazen threshold rose above the steps, [2]

---

[1] Lane's *Thousand and One Nights,* Notes to Chapter 3, Vol. I., p 215f. See, also, Stanley Lane's *Arabian Society in the Middle Ages,* p. 73.

[2] Or, "by steps,"--"*gradibus.*"

With brazen posts connecting, and the hinge
Creaked upon brazen doors."[1]

The churches of Abyssinia always stand on a hill, and in a grove—like the temple at Carthage. "When you go to the church you put off your shoes before your first entering the outer precinct . . . At entry, you kiss the threshold and two door-posts, go in and say what prayer you please; that finished you come out again, and your duty is over."[2]

The yard of an Abyssinian church has been compared to "the *lucus* or sacred grove of the pagan temple." "The church itself is square, and built of stone with beams stuck in to support them. At the porch, the wooden lintels, which the pious kiss with intense earnestness,—in fact, kissing the walls and lintels of a church is great feature in Abyssinian devotion, so much so that, instead of speaking of 'going to church,' they say 'kissing the church,'—are carved with quaint and elaborate devices."[3]

At Yeha, near Aksum, are the remains of a ruined temple, within the area of which a church was at one time built. "In front of the vestibule stood two rude monoliths, at the base of one of which is an altar with a circular disk on it, presumably, from the analogy of those at Aksum, for receiving the blood of slaughtered victims." Obviously, the altar of this temple was at its threshold.

Marriages are said to be celebrated in Abyssinia at the

---

[1] Cranch's *Aeneid of Virgil*, I., 572-585; *Aeneis*, I., 441-449.

[2] Bruce's *Travels* (Dublin ed.), III., 644, Bk. IV., chap. 12.

[3] Bent's *Sacred City of the Ethiopians*, p. 40f.

church door—the wedding covenant being thus made before the threshold altar.[1]

And so in the earlier temples of Egypt, of Carthage, and of Abyssinia, and in Christian and Muhammadan places of worship, the doorway is held sacred, and, most of all, the threshold, or "floor of the door."

5. TEMPLE THRESHOLDS IN EUROPE.

Traces of the primitive sacredness of the doorway and the threshold, in places of worship, are to be found in Europe, ancient and modern, as in Asia and Africa.

The term "threshold" occurs in such prominence in connection with temples, in the earliest Greek literature, as to show that its primitive meaning included the idea of altar, or of sanctuary foundation. Thus the House of Zeus on Olympus is repeatedly spoken of as the "House of the Bronze Threshold."[2] In these references, "the nature of the occurrences, the uniformity of the phrase, the position of the words in the verse, all point to this as an old hieratic phrase, and the meaning evidently is 'the house that is stablished forever.'"[3]

This term "bronze threshold" occurs more than once in

---

[1] See Wood's *Wedding Day in All Ages and Countries*, II., 17.

[2] See, for example, *Iliad*, I., 426; XIV., 173; XXI., 427, 505; *Odyssey*, VIII., 321.

[3] Professor W. A. Lamberton, in a personal note to the author.

reference to the temple-palace of Aleinous.[1] Tartarus is described as having gates of iron and a "bronze threshold."[2] Night and day meet as they cross the "great threshold of bronze;" and Atlas up-holds heaven at the threshold of the under-world.[3]

The treasures of Delphi are described as "within the stone threshold of the archer god, Phoebus Apollo, in Rocky Pytho."[4] And he who seeks counsel at that oracle is spoken of as one who crosses "the stone threshold."[5]

In Sophocles' "Oedipus at Colonus" the Athenian warns the stranger Oedipus that he is on holy ground, in the realm of Poseidon, and that the spot where he now treads is "called the brazen threshold of the land, the stay of Athens."[6] In other words, the bronze threshold is an archaic synonym for the enduring border, or outer limit, of spiritual domain.

This prominence given to the threshold in earlier Greek literature is not, it is true, continued in later writings; yet there are traces of it still in occasional poetic references to the "threshold of life," and the "threshold of the year," and the "threshold of old age." When Homer refers "to houses,

---

[1] *Odyssey*, XIII., 4; VII., 83, 87, 89.

[2] *Iliad*, VIII., 15.

[3] See Hesiod's *Theogony*, V., 749.

[4] *Iliad*, IX., 404.

[5] *Odyssey*, VIII., 80.

[6] *Oedipus at Colonus*, 54ff. See, also, I 591. Comp. Hesiod's *Theogony*, 811.

to rooms in houses, or to courtyards, the 'threshold' is constantly spoken of: a man steps over a threshold, stands at a threshold, sits at a threshold, etc. And so important is the threshold that its material is almost regularly mentioned; it is ash, oak, stone, bronze, etc. In later times all these locutions disappear; men go through doorways, enter, stand in porches, etc., instead."[1] Yet it is the archaic use that points to the primitive prominence of the threshold.

In historic times, however, as in earlier, the altar of sacrifice was to be found, in Grecian and Roman temples, near the threshold of the door. While there were smaller altars, for the offering of incense and bloodless sacrifices, in the interior of temples, the larger and more important altars, for the offering of animal sacrifices, whether of beasts or of men, were before the temple, in front of the threshold,—*bomoi pronàoi*.[2]

A ruined temple of Artemis Propylaea, at Eleusis, shows the main altar immediately before the threshold, between the antae. The altar of the temple of Apollo at Delphi was in a like position as shown in the fact that "when Neoptolemus is attacked by Orestes in the vestibule of the temple at Delphi, he seizes the arms which were suspended by means of nails or pins from one of the antae, takes his station upon the altar, and addresses the people in

---

[1] Prof. W. A. Lamberton.

[2] Aeschylus's "Suppliants," p. 497; cited in Smith's *Dict. Of Greek and Roman Antiq.*, s.v."Ara." See, also, Donaldson's *Architectura Numismatica*, pp. xvi, xvii, 33, 54.

his own defense."[1]

When the "priest of Jupiter, whose temple was before the city" of Lystra, would have given diving honors to Paul and Barnabas, he brought the garlanded oxen "unto the gates," to sacrifice them there. At the gate of the city, within which the supposed gods were to be found, seemed the proper place of sacrifice.[2]

There are references in classic story, as in Babylonian legends, in Phenician and Syrian beliefs, and in the Hebrew prophetic visions, to life-giving waters flowing out from under the threshold of the sanctuary. In the garden of the palace-temple of Aleinous "are two springs, the one ripples through the whole garden, the other opposite it gushes under the threshold of the courtyard to the lofty house, and from it the citizens draw their water."[3] On "the apple-growing shores of the Hesperides," where Atlas upholds "the holy threshold of heaven," according to the poets, "springs of ambrosia pour from the chamber of Zeus, from his bedside," and give a rich blessing to the life-giving earth.[4] And of Delphi it is said: "Going toward the temple we come upon the spring Cassotis: there is a low wall about it, and you ascend to the spring through the walls. The water of this Cassotis they say sinks underground, and in the shrine of the god [Apollo] makes the woman prophet-

---

[1] Euripides, *Androm*., 1098. Smith's *Dict. of Greek and Rom. Antiq.*, s.v. "Antae."

[2] Acts 14:8-14.

[3] *Odyssey*, VII., 130.

[4] Euripides, *Hippolytus*, 741.

ic [is inspiration to her.]"[1]

In the early churches of Europe, the threshold marked a sacred boundary of the edifice, to cross which indicated a certain covenant right to participate in the privileges of the house of God. As the structure of the churches changed, in the progress of the centuries, the threshold of the sanctuary came to be in a different portion of the building, or series of buildings; but its sacredness remained, wherever it was supposed to be. The term "altar" also changed, from the border line of the place of worship, to the holy table within the sanctuary.

Speaking of the growth of the early church buildings, Bingham says: "In the strictest sense, including only the buildings within the walls, they were commonly divided into three parts: (1.) The *narthex* or ante-temple, where the penitents and catechumens stood. (2.) The *naos* or temple, where the communicants had their respective places. And (3) the *bema* or sanctuary, where the clergy stood to officiate at the altar. But in a larger sense there was another ante-temple or *narthex* without the walls, under which was comprised the propylaea, or *vestibulium,* the outward porch; then the *atrium* or area, the court leading from that to the temple, surrounded with porticos or cloisters . . . There were also several *exedrae*, such as the batosterum the *diaconcium*, the *pastophoria*, and other adjacent buildings, which were reckoned to be either without or within the church, according as it was taken in a stricter or a larger

---

[1] *Pausanias,* Bk. X., 24, 5.

acception."[1]

In the early churches, the place of baptism was outside of the church proper, or the *naos,* it is said. "There is nothing more certain than that for many ages the baptistery was a distinct place from the body of the church, and reckoned among the *exedrae,* or places adjoining to the church."[2] The first ages all agreed in this, that, whether they had baptisteries or not, the place of baptism was always without the church."[3] Even in mediaeval times, in the churches of England, baptisms were on the outer side of the threshold of the church proper, "the child being held without the doors of the church"[4] until baptized. In many churches of Europe at the present time the baptismal font is at or near the door of the church.

In 1661, a formal reply of the Church of England bishops to a request of the Presbyterians that the font might be placed before the congregation, that all might see it, was: "The font usually stands, as it did in primitive times, at or near the church door, to signify that baptism was the entrance into the church mystical."[5]

Marriages, like baptisms, were at the church porch or outside of the threshold. "The old missals direct the placing of the man and the woman at the church door during the

---

[1] Bingham's *Antiquities of the Christian Church,* Bk. VIII., chap. 3.

[2] *Ibid.,* Bk. VIII., chap. 4.

[3] *Ibid.* Bk. VIII., chap. 7.

[4] Blunt's *Annotated Book of Common Prayer,* p. 210.

[5] *Ibid.,* p. 217.

125

service, and that at the end of it they shall proceed within up to the altar."[1] The idea would seem to be that a holy covenant like marriage, which is the foundation of a new family, must be solemnized at the primitive family altar,—the threshold.

Describing the marriage rites of Germany in the middle ages, Baring-Gould says: "In a Ritual of Rennes, of the eleventh century, we find a rubric to this effect: 'The priest shall go before the door of the church in surplice and stole, and ask the bridegroom and bride prudently whether they desire to be legally united; and then he shall make the parents give her away, according to the usual custom, and the bridegroom shall fix the dower, announcing before all present what (witthum) he intends to give the bride. Then the priest shall make him betroth her with a ring, and give her an honorarium of gold or silver according to his means. Then let him give the prescribed benediction. After which, entering into the church, let him begin mass; and let the bridegroom and bride hold lighted candles, and make an oblation at the offertory; and before the Pax let the priest bless them before the altar under a pall or other covering [the wedding canopy], according to custom; and lastly, let the bridegroom receive the kiss of peace from the priest, and pass it on to his bride.'"[2]

"In ancient times the people of France were married, not within the church at the altar as now, but at the outer door. This was the case in 1599, in which year Elizabeth,

---

[1] See Wood's *Wedding Day in All Ages and Countries*, II., 15f.

[2] Baring-Gould's *Germany, Present and Past* (Am. Ed) p. 195.

the daughter of Henry II., was married to Philip II of Spain; and the Bishop of Paris performed the ceremony at the door of the cathedral of Notre Dame. Another instance of this kind occurred in 1599 in France. Henrietta Maria was married to King Charles by proxy at the door of Notre Dame, and the bride, as soon as the ceremony was over entered the church, and assisted at [attended] mass."[1]

"The pre-Reformation rule was to begin the marriage service at the door of the church. In his 'Wyf of Bathe,' Chaucer [in the days of Edward III.] refers to this custom:—

'Housbandes atte chirche dore I have had fyve.'

This old usage was abandoned by authority in the time of Edward VI. Yet there is reason for thinking that it was not entirely given up. "There is a poem of Herrick's, written about 1640, which is entitled, 'The Entertainment or Porch Verse at the Marriage of Mr. Hen. Northly.'"[2]

"When Edward I married Marguerite of France, in 1299, he endowed her at the door of Canterbury Cathedral." Selden declares that "dower could be lawfully assigned only at the door;" and Littleton affirms to the same effect.[3]

"At Witham in Essex it is, or was, the custom to perform the first part of the marriage service at the font [near the door]. When the Rev. A. Snell was appointed to the benefice in 1873, he spoke to a bridegroom about this

---

[1] Wood's *Wedding Day in All Ages and Countries*, II., 14f.

[2] Vaux's *Church Folk-Lore*, p. 99.

[3] Wood's *Wedding Day in All Ages and Countries*, II., 16.

usage, and he (the bridegroom) particularly requested that he might be married at the font, as he liked old customs."[1]

Another survival of the primitive rite of threshold covenanting seems to be shown in certain customs observed in various parts of Europe, which look like the substitution of an altar-stone for a threshold altar, in the marriage ceremony.

"Thus in the old temple of Upsal (in Sweden), wedding couples stood upon a broad stone which was believed to cover the tomb of St. Eric"[2] Corresponding customs in other regions would go to show that the earlier practice was to leap over the stone, as a mode of threshold covenanting, instead of standing on it. The latter was a change without a reason for it.

For instance, just outside "the ruined church, or abbey, of Lindisfarne, is the socket or foot-stone, in which was mortised a ponderous stone cross, erected by Ethelwold, and broken down by the Danes. This socket stone is now called the "petting stone," and whenever a marriage is solemnized in the neighborhood, after the ceremony the bride is obliged to step upon it; and if she cannot stride to the end thereof, the marriage is deemed likely to prove unfortunate and fruitless." While this would seem to point to the custom of standing upon the stone, in the modern marriage customs of the same region, a barrier is "erected at the churchyard gate, consisting of a large paving stone which was placed on its edge and supported by two smaller stones. On either side

---

[1] Vaux's *Church Folk-Lore,* p. 98.

[2] Wood's *Wedding Day in All Ages and Countries,* II., 17.

stood a villager, who made the couple and everyone else jump over it."[1]

"In Lantevit Major Church was a stone called the 'marriage stone,' with many knots and flourishes, and the head of a person upon it, and this inscription:

> 'Ne Petra calcetur
> Qu[a]e subjacet ista tuetur.'

Brides usually stood upon this stone at their marriages."[2] Yet the inscription itself:

> "Let not the stone be trodden upon;
> What it lies under, it guards."

forbids standing upon this threshold altar; and it is probable that in earlier times it was stepped over in marriage covenant, and not upon.

At Belford, in Northumberland, it is still the custom to make the bridal pair, with their attendants, leap over a stone placed in their path outside the church porch. This stone also is called the "petting stone," or the "louping stone." At the neighboring village of Embleton, in the same county, two stout young lads place a wooden bench across the door of the church porch, and assist the bride and groom and their attendants to surmount the obstacle; for which assistance a gift of money is expected. In some places a

---

[1] Wood's *Wedding Day in All Ages and Countries*, II., 254.

[2] Wood's *Wedding Day in All Ages and Countries*, II., 255.

129

stick has been held by the groomsmen at the church door for the bride to jump over. And again a stool has been placed at the churchyard gate, over which the whole bridal party must jump one by one; and this stool has been called the "parting-stool."[1]

A "mode of marriage" current in Ireland, until recent times, was that of jumping over a form of the cross;[2] and jumping over a broomstick as a form of marriage would seem to be a survival of this custom of leaping across the threshold-stone, in token of a covenant. "Jumping the broomstick" is sometimes spoken of as an equivalent of marriage.

These various obstacles to progress, at wedding time, would seem to be as suggestions of the threshold altar, which must be passed in the marriage covenant. The church threshold, like the home threshold, is a temporary hindrance to an advance. Unless it is stepped across, the covenant is incomplete.

An illustration of the popular idea of the sacredness of the church threshold, and of the impropriety of stepping on it, in its passing, is found in a Finnish mode of judging a clergyman. "In Finland, it is regarded as unlucky if a clergyman steps on the threshold, when he comes to preach at a church." A writer on this subject says: "A Finnish friend told me of one of his relations going to preach at a church, a few years ago,—he being a candidate for the

---

[1] See Henderson's *Folk-Lore of the Northern Counties of England and the Borders,* p. 38.

[2] Curtin's *Myths and Folk-Lore of Ireland,* p. 177.

vacant living,—and the people most anxiously watched if he stepped on the threshold as he came in. Had he done so, I fear a sermon never so eloquent would have counted but little against so dire an omen."[1] Here is a new peril for pulpit candidates, if this primitive test becomes widely popular!

Even to the present time, it is customary, in portions of Europe, for Jews to rub their fingers on the posts of a synagogue doorway, and then kiss their fingers. Quite an indentation in the stone at the door of the synagogue in Worms is to be seen, as due to this constant sacred rubbing.[2]

6. TEMPLE THRESHOLDS IN AMERICA.

In the West, as in the East, traces of the primitive sacredness of the threshold and the doorway are to be found. The stepped pyramid, or uplifted threshold, with the sanctuary at its summit, was the earliest form of temple or place of worship in Mexico, and in Central and South America. In the later and more elaborate temples there was no altar within the building, although an image of the god was there.

The altar, or stone of sacrifice, was without, before the door of the sanctuary. [3] When a sacrifice was offered on the

---

[1]   See Jones' and Knopf's *Folk-Tales of the Magyars*, p. 410.

[2]   On the eye witness testimony of Prof. Dr. Morris Jastrow, Jr.

[3]   Reville's *Nat. Relig. Of Mex. And Peru*, pp. 41, 179f., 207; also Banc-roft's *Mex.*, I., 296.

altar, the blood of that sacrifice was smeared on the doors of
the temple of the god.[1] Human sacrifices were included in
these offerings, in earlier times.[2] Even when larger temples
were erected, and altars were enclosed within them, human
victims were brought to the temple entrance into the hands
of the priests; and from the threshold they were borne by the
priests themselves, to be laid on the altar.[3]

Among the Pipiles, a Maya people, in Central America,
there were "two principal and very solemn sacrifices; one at
the commencement of summer, and the other at the beginning of winter." Little boys, from six to twelve years old,
were the victims of sacrifice. At the sound of trumpets and
drums, which assembled the people, four priests came out
of the temple with braziers of coals on which incense was
burning, and after various ceremonies and religious exercises they proceeded to the house of the high-priest, near the
temple, and took from it the boy victim of the sacrifice. He
was then conducted four times round the court of the
temple, with dancing and singing.

When this ceremony was finished, the high-priest came
out of his house with the second priest and his major-domo,
and they proceeded to the temple steps, accompanied by the
principal men of the locality, who, however, stopped at the
threshold of the temple. Then and there the four priests
"seized the victim by his extremities, and the major-domo
coming out, with little bells on his wrists and ankles,

---

[1] Reville's *Nat. Relig. Of Mex. And Peru*, p. 183; Bancroft's *Mex.*, I., 162.

[2] Reville's *Nat. Relig. Of Mex. And Peru*, pp. 31, 184, 207f.

[3] *Ibid.* p. 83.

opened the left breast of the boy, tore out his heart, and handed it to the high-priest, who put it into a little embroidered purse, which he closed."

The blood of the victim was received by the priests in a vessel made of a gourd, and was by them sprinkled in the direction of the four cardinal points. Then the heart, in its purse, was put back into the body of the victim, and the body itself was interred inside of the temple. This sacrifice, at the threshold altar, was performed at the threshold, or the beginning, of each of the two chief seasons of the year.[1]

In the temples of Central America, generally, the doorway was hardly less prominent than in the temples of Egypt. There were massive decorations on and above the lintels; the door jams were richly sculptured; and there were male and female figures, or figures of animals, as guardians on either side of the entrance. In some instances a winged globe was above the door; and the uplifted hand was found over the doorway or at the sides.[2]

Among the Natchez Indians, along the lower Mississippi, there was an annual "Harvest Festival," or "festival of New Fire." which was celebrated with great ceremony. An altar was in front of the temple, just before the door. On this occasion the priest of the sun stood on the threshold of the temple in the early morning, watching for the first rays of the rising sun. The chiefs, and braves old

---

[1] Bancroft's *Native Races*, "Civilized Nations," II., 706f.

[2] See Bancroft's *Native Races* and *Antiquities*, IV., 209f., 314, 321, 323, 332, 338, 351, 531, 801, 805. See also, Stephens' *Incidents of Travels in Yucatan*, I., 137, 167-176, 303, 306, 403-407, 411-413, II., 42, 54, 56, 72, 122.

and young, stood near the altar. The women with infants in their arms stood in a semicircle facing the priest. When he gave the signal of his recognition of the sun, by rubbing two pieces of wood to start a new fire for the altar, they faced about to the east and held up their infants to the sun. Other exercises of worship followed. The priest's place in this ceremony was on the threshold, before the altar of that temple.[1]

In America, as in the other continents, there are survivals of the primal sacredness of the threshold of a place of public worship, in the formal ceremonies attending the laying of the cornerstone, or threshold-stone, of a new church building of any denomination; and in the use of holy water at the doorway on entering Roman Catholic churches. More or less importance is attached in Protestant Episcopal churches to the location of the baptismal font near the door, and to the beginning of the marriage service before the bridal party approaches the threshold of the sanctuary proper.

If indeed, there be found no trace of the fountain of life flowing from under the threshold sanctuary of the gods worshiped by the aborigines of America, such a fountain was searched for in this land by Ponce de Leon and his followers.

---

[1] Chateaubrand's *Voyage En Amerique*, pp. 130-136; cited in Frazer's *Golden Bough*, II., 383.

7. TEMPLE THRESHOLDS IN ISLANDS OF THE SEA.

There is a certain resemblance in the plan of some of the temples of the South Sea Islands to those of Central America. A stepped pyramid in a large court was the central shrine; "in front of which the images were kept, and the altars fixed,"[1] In both cases the altars were outside of the shrine,—at its threshold, as it were. A method of sacrificing was by bleeding a pig to death before the altar, "washing the carcass with the blood, and then placing it in a crouching position on the altar."[2] An uplifted hand was one of the symbols on these stepped pyramid shrines.[3] The temple foundation, or the threshold of the sacred building, was formerly laid in human blood.[4]

A recognition of the threshold, in a sacred service, and in a form of covenanting, is found in the ceremonies of circumcision as observed in Madagascar. This rite is not at infancy, as among the Jews, but is at the threshold of young manhood. Its period is fixed by the king, who, on "an application from the parents or the friends of any number of children in a given province, appoints a time, and orders the observance of the rite." He is the "high-priest on this occasion." The rite marks the transition of the boy from his

---

[1] Ellis' *Polynesian Researches*, II., 206.

[2] *Ibid.*, II., 211f.

[3] *Ibid.* II., 207, illustration.

[4] *Ibid.* II. 212f.

dependence on his parents to his personal service to the king, as a member of the community.

Holy water is brought from a distance to the house of the master of ceremonies, as the sanctuary for the occasion. A sheep is killed immediately before this house, and the boys are caused to step across its blood. This sacrifice is called "fahazza," or "causing fruitfulness," and it is supposed to be the means of causing fruitfulness in all the women who obtain a share of it.

A tree is planted at the northeast corner of the house, and a lamp is fixed on it. Honey and water are poured upon the tree, and the boys partake of this mixture. The next day the persons present walk three times round the house, with various ceremonies, and then stop at the doorway. The rite of circumcision is performed on each boy as he sits on a drum at "the threshold of the door," held firmly by several men. The knife with which it is performed is previously dipped in the blood of a young bullock, an ear of which is slit by the operator. A covenant of fealty to the king is entered into by the youth on this occasion. Sacrifices and feasting follow this ceremony.[1]

One of the ancient gods of Maui, an island of Hawaii, was Keoroeva. "In all the temples dedicated to its worship, the image was placed within the inner apartment, on the left-hand side of the door; and immediately before it stood the altar, on which the offerings of every kind were usually placed."[2] The altar was at the doorway, in this case, as so

---

[1] Ellis' *Hist. Of Madagascar*, I., 176-187.

[2] Ellis' *Through Hawaii*, p. 73f.

generally elsewhere. Tiha was a female idol, as Keoroeva was a male, and much "the same homage and offerings" were given to her as to him.[1]

In Kohala, one of the large divisions of Hawaii, stood a prominent temple called Bukohola, built by King Kamehameha, at the time of his conquest of the Sandwich Islands. "At the south end of this great edifice was a kind of inner court, which might be called the *sanctum sanctorum* of the temple, where the principal idol used to stand, surrounded by a number of images of inferior deities." "On the outside, near the entrance to the inner court [at the threshold of the *sanctum sanctorum*] was the place of the *rere* [or *lele]* (altar), on which human and other sacrifices were offered.[2]

Human victims were ordinarily slain in sacrifice outside of the sanctuary proper, and then their bodies, carefully preserved whole, were taken within to be presented to the idol.[3]

There were Hawaiian cities of refuge or *puhonnas*, as sanctuaries for guilty fugitives. A thief, or a murderer, might be pursued to the very gateway of one of those cities, but as soon as he crossed the threshold of that gate, even though the gates were open, and no barrier hindered pursuit, he was safe, as at the city altar. When once within the sacred city, the fugitive's first duty was to present himself before the

---

[1] Ibid., p. 75.

[2] Ellis' *Through Hawaii*, p. 81f.

[3] *Ibid* .p. 135f; also, Isabella Bird's *Six Months in the Sandwich Islands*, p. 196.

idol, and return thanks for his protection.[1] This was substantially the Hebrew law as to the cities of refuge.[2] Safety was only within the threshold.

There are traces of the primitive idea of a spring of life-giving waters flowing from under the threshold of the goddess of life, in the Islands of the Sea. According to the myths of that region, Vari, or "The-very-beginning" of life was a woman. She plucked off a piece of her right side and it became a man, or part man and part fish, known as Vatea, or Avatea. From the under-world there came to Vatea a supernatural woman called Papa, or Foundation. From this union the human race began. Rongo was the first-born son. The Hades of Polynesia is Avaika, or Hawaika. In the days of Rongo, and later, there was an opening from earth to Avaika; but because of the misdoings of the denizens of that realm, coming up through that passage-way, Tiki, a lovely woman, a descendant of Rongo, "rolled herself alive down into the gloomy opening, which immediately closed upon her." She was the first to die. And now "Tiki sits at the threshold" of her home below, to welcome the descendants of Rongo, who bring her an offering. A sacred stream of water, "Vairorongo," comes up from below into the sacred grove devoted to the worship of Rongo, and near that stream it is possible for a spirit to be returned to life and to a home

---

[1] Ellis' *Through Hawaii*, p .155f. See also, Isabella Bird's *Six Months in the Sandwich Islands*, p 135f.

[2] Num. 35:6-32; Deut. 4:41-43; 19:1-13; Josh. 20:1-9

on earth again.[1]

It is obvious that the idea of the sacredness of the threshold, in home, in temple, or in sanctuary, is not of any one time or of any one people, but is of human nature as human nature everywhere. It shows itself all the world over, and always. And it has to do with life, and its perpetuation or reproduction.

8. ONLY ONE FOUNDATION.

An idea tangent to, rather than identical with, the thought of the altar sacredness of the temple threshold, as found among primitive peoples, is that the first temple foundation is the foundation for all subsequent temple building at that place. And it has already been shown that the threshold, or hearthstone, or cornerstone, is considered the foundation.[2]

In ancient Babylonia a temple, however grand and extensive, was supposed to be built on the foundation of an earlier temple; the one threshold being the first threshold and the latest. If, indeed, there was a variation from the original foundation in the construction of a new temple, there was confusion and imperfectness in consequence, and the only hope of reformation was in finding the first temple threshold and rebuilding it.

---

[1] Comp. Gill's *Myths and Songs from the South Pacific*, pp. 3, 4, 7, 14. 18, 20, 26, 152, 155, 158, 160, 170; also Turner's *Samoa*, p. 259.

[2] See pp. 21-23, 45f., 55, supra.

There is an illustration of this in an inscription discovered in the foundation of a temple at "Ur of the Chaldees."[1] Nabonidus (556-538 B.C.), the last Babylonian king, tells with interest of his search for the old foundation, or outline plan, of the ancient temple, Eulbar, or, more properly, Eulmash, of the goddess Istar of Agade, as follows:[2]

The foundation of Eulmash in Agade had not been found from Sargon, king of Babylon (3800 B.C.), and Naram-Sin, his son, kings living formerly, until the government of Nabuna'id king of Babylon.

King Kurigalzu (II.), about 1300 B.C., had, in his reign, searched for this foundation, but had failed to find it, and he had left this record: "The foundation of Eulmash I sought, but did not find it." Later on, Esarhaddon, king of Assyria and Babylonia (681-669 B.C.) searched for it, but without success. Again, Nebuchadrezzar (605-561 B.C.) mobilized his large armies, and ordered them to search for the foundation stone, or threshold, but all his efforts were in vain. Finally Nabuna'id, the last king of Babylon before its fall under Cyrus, gathered his many soldiers, and ordered them to search for the foundation stone. For "three years in the tracks of Nebuchadrezzar king of Babylon," says Nabunaid, "I sought right and left, before and behind, but did not find it."

Encouraged by a prompting from the moon-god Sin, Nabuna'id tried at another time and in another place, and

---

[1] Gen. 11:28; Neh. 9:7.

[2] Rawlinson's *Inscript. Of W. Asia*, Vol.I., pl. 69, Col. II., I. 29ff.

this time with success. He found the inscription of King Shjagarakti-Buriash (1350 B.C.), which tells that he had laid a new foundation exactly upon the old one of King Zabû (about 2300 B.C.). Then Nabuna'id made sure to preserve the exact outline of the old shrine. He laid the foundation, and restored the ancient temple, so that "it did not deviate an inch to the outside or the inside."[1]

There are indications of the same high value set upon the primal foundation of a temple in the records of ancient Egypt. A temple at its highest grandeur is in the location of a prehistoric sanctuary. "The site on which it is built is generally *holy ground*,[2] that is, a spot on which since the memory of man an older sanctuary of the god had stood. Even those Egyptian temples which seem most modern have usually a long history,—the edifice may have seemed very insignificant, but as the prestige of the god increased larger buildings were erected, which again, in the course of centuries, were enlarged and rebuilt in such a way that the original plan could no longer be traced. This is history of nearly all Egyptian temples, and explains the fact that we know so little of the temples of the Old and of the Middle Empire; they have all been metamorphosed into the vast buildings of the New Empire."[3]

While early Vedic and Brahmanic religion makes no mention of temples as such, fire from an ancestral altar was borne to a newly erected altar, in order to secure a continu-

---

[1] See Hilprecht's *Assyriaca*, pp. 54, 55, 97.

[2] Inscription in the temple of Rameses III. at Karnak.

[3] Erman's *Life in Ancient Egypt*, p. 279.

ance of the sacred influences issuing from that original family threshold. [1] And Vishnooism takes old temples from Booddhism for its centers of worship, prizing the old sacred foundation.

"Buddha-Gaya," or "Bodhi-Gaya," in Upper India, is famous as the locality of the holy pipal tree, or the Booddha-drum ("Tree of Knowledge"), under which for six years sat Sakya Sinha, in meditation, before he attained to Booddha-hood. A temple still standing on that site is supposed to have been rebuilt A.D. 1306, on the remains of one visited by Hwen Thsang, a Chinese traveler, in the seventh century of our era, which, in turn, had been built by Amara Sinha, or Amara Deva, about A.D. 500. This earlier temple is said to have been built by a command of Booddha himself conveyed in a vision, or by a command of the Brahmanical Mahâdeva, on the site of a still earlier sanctuary, or monastery, erected by Asoka between 259 and 241 B.C., on the site of Booddha's meditations, about 300 B.C.[2] The existing temple has been called at different times "Buddha-pad" and "Vishnu-pad, "Booddha's foot" and "Vishnoo's foot."

Kuru-Kshetra, or the "Plain of Kuru," near Delhi, India, has been deemed holy ground from time immemorial. At Thâvesar, on this plain, a temple of Siva was built on a site that was sacred long before Sivaism was known. It is even

---

[1] See "Grihya-Sutras," in *Sacred Books of the East*, XXX.,193-201; also De Coulange's *Ancient City*, pp. 36, 47f.

[2] See Julien's *Memoires de Hionen-thsang*, I., 459-466; Cunningham's *Archaeological Survey of India*, I., 1-12; Sir Monier Monier-Williams' Buddhism, pp. 390-401.

believed that the sacredness of this site runs back to the ancient times of the Rig Veda. The boundaries of this "Holy Land" are given in the great Hindoo epic, the Mahabharata. This plain is said to comprise three hundred and sixty holy shrines, each of which is erected on a foundation sacred from the times of the gods themselves.[1]

So general, in India, is this habit of building a sanctuary on an old sacred foundation, that it is said that "the erection of a mosk by a Muhammadan conqueror always implies the previous destruction of a Hindu temple."[2] Thus a mosk erected by the emperor Altamash, A.D. 1232, is supposed to have been on the foundation of a temple of the sun, built for Raja Pasupati about A.D. 300.[3] Not a new foundation, but an old one, was sought, in India, for a new temple, even to a god newly worshiped there.

Fourteen centuries before Christ, Pan-Kăng, an emperor of China, moved his capital from north of the Ho to south of it, because he had ascertained that the original foundation was attempted to be laid there by his ancestor Thang in the Shing dynasty, seventeen reigns before him; hence the removal back to that first foundation would renew the blessing of Thang upon his descendants.[4]

A temple has added sacredness in China according as its foundation is on a spot originally chosen or honored by

---

[1] Cunningham's *Archaeological Survey of India*, II., 212, 213.

[2] *Ibid.* II., 353f.

[3] *Ibid.*

[4] "The Shih King,"Bk.7. §3, in *Sacred Books of the East*, III., iii.

a representative of Heaven as a threshold of a place of worship. Thus Tai Shan, or the "Great Mount," in the province of Shantung, China, is mentioned in the Shoo King, or Book of Records, as the site of the great Emperor Shun's altar of sacrifice to Heaven, 2254 B.C., or, say, three centuries before the time of Abraham. On this holy mountain, as the earliest historic foundation of Chinese worship, "is the great rendezvous of devotees, every sect has there its temples and idols, scattered up and down its sides;" and great multitudes come thither to worship from near and far.[1]

This idea shows itself in modern discoveries among the ruins of ancient Greece. It appears that when Pericles (437 B.C.) began his building of the new Propylaea on the Acropolis, he would have cleared away the remains of such ancient sacred structures as stood within its outline. "The plan of Mnesikles the architect was very simple, and is still clear enough, though it was never fully carried out." "That the original plan of Mnesikles had undergone modifications was long ago seen by every architect who made the Propylaea matter of serious study." Dr. Dörpfeld thinks he has discovered how the plan was modified, and why. The enforced departure from the original plan seems to have been because that plan involved the destruction of shrines on an earlier foundation, with a threshold that might not be moved. The gate of Cimon, with its "statue of some guardian god of the gate,—it may be Hermes Propylaios himself,"—was within that outline, and also other sacred sites.

---

[1] Williams' *Middle Kingdom,* I., 96f.

"Against such intrusion it is very likely the priesthood rose and protested, and, before even the foundations were laid, he had to give up, at least for the time, the whole of the southeast hall, and a part of the southwest wing." This conclusion is the result of recent investigation by careful scholars, and it is in accordance with the ascertained fact that in primitive thought an original foundation for a temple or shrine is counted sacred for all time as the foundation there for such a place of worship, not to be swept away or ignored in any rebuilding or new building.[1]

When from any reason, in early Europe, an ancient shrine must be removed from its primitive foundation, it was deemed desirable to remove to the new site a portion of the foundation itself, as well as the sanctuary or altar above that foundation. Thus, for example, when Thorolf of Norway, who had charge of the temple of Thor in Mostur, removed to Iceland in A. D. 833, he took with him the temple posts and furniture "and the very earth on which the altar of that idol had been erected." And when he landed in Iceland, Thorolf built a new temple of Thor, with an altar on the foundation which he had brought from the earlier shrine. A thousand years after this the foundation-site of that second temple was still pointed out near Hofstad, in Iceland.[2]

Bible language and narrative abound with incidental evidence of the commonness of this primitive idea. When Jacob, on his way to Haran, came to Beth-el—a House of

---

[1] Harrison and Verrall's *Myth, and Monu. Of Anc. Athens*, pp. 353-361.

[2] Henderson's *Iceland*, II., 64-67; also ibid., I., xiv.

God—he lighted on "the place." (*hammaqâm)* where,[1] long before, his ancestor Abraham had worshiped, as he came from Egypt by way of the Negeb.[2] And yet earlier Abraham himself, as he came a pilgrim from Haran and Ur, had there "builded an altar unto the Lord, and called upon the name of the Lord."[3] And if that place were already known as Beth-el it must have been a sanctuary before Abraham's day.

Moses, in the wilderness of Sinai, is told that the ground whereon he stands is "holy ground," and that he is to bring the Hebrews out of Egypt to worship God in that mountain.[4] And the Egyptian records give reason for supposing that that region of Mt. Sinai, perhaps of the moon-god "Sin," was known as holy ground, and as the "land of God," or of the gods, before the days of Moses.[5]

At Jerusalem the Temple was built on Mt. Moriah, where the ark of the covenant rested after its return from Philistia,[6] and where David erected an altar to the Lord after the staying of the pestilence from Israel.[7] And it is supposed that this same Mt. Moriah was where Abraham offered a

---

[1] Gen. 28:10-22.

[2] *Ibid.*, 13:1-3.

[3] *Ibid.* 12:1-8.

[4] Exod. 3:1-12.

[5] Brugsch's *Egypt under the Pharaohs*, I., 411.

[6] II Sam. 6:1-19.

[7] *Ibid.*, 24:15-25.

sacrifice to God on an altar he had built for the sacrifice of his son.[1] And this site of the Temple at Jerusalem is held sacred today, in view of its being deemed by multitudes a holy place from the beginning of the world.[2]

When Naaman the Syrian was healed of leprosy by Elisha, the prophet of Israel, he desired thenceforth to worship Jehovah in his Syrian home. To this end he asked of Elisha the gift of "two mules' burden of earth" from Samaria, in order that he might on that sacred foundation erect in Syria an altar to Jehovah.[3]

In a prophecy of the Messiah as the foundation, or threshold, of a new temple, it was declared by the Lord: "Behold, I lay [or I have laid] in Zion for a foundation a stone, a tried stone, a precious cornerstone of sure foundation."[4] Again, it was the promise of God to the Israelites that they should be restorers of worship on former foundations. "They that shall be of thee shall build the old waste places: thou shalt raise up the foundations of many generations; and thou shalt be called The repairer of the breach, The restorer of paths to dwell in."[5]

New Testament phraseology makes frequent reference to this same idea. "According to the grace which was given

---

[1] Gen. 22:1-13.

[2] As evidenced in the traditional claim that the grave of Adam was under the cross.

[3] II Kings 5:17.

[4] Isa. 28:16; I Pet. 2:6.

[5] Isa. 58:12.

unto me, as a wise master-builder, I laid a foundation," says Paul. "But let each man take heed how he buildeth thereon. For other foundation can no man lay than that is laid, which is Christ Jesus."[1] The Christian saints of the "household of God," as "living stones,"[2] are "built upon the foundation of the apostles and prophets, Christ Jesus himself being the chief cornerstone; in whom each several building, fitly framed together, groweth into a holy temple in the Lord."[3]

Muhammadanism, which shows many survivals of primitive ideas and primitive customs, emphasizes the importance of the first foundation as the only foundation, in the traditions and legends of the holy places of its most sacred city. Every *masjid,* or "place of prostration," in that vicinity is on a site counted holy long centuries before the days of the Prophet of Islam.

The Ka'bah, or Holy House, in the mosk at Mecca is said to have been built by Adam himself, on the model of a similar structure in heaven. It would seem as if no earthly foundation, or threshold, could have been earlier than that; indeed, the Qurân declares: "The first house appointed unto men to worship in was that which was in Beccah [or Meccah];[4] yet there is a tradition that Adam erected a place of prayer even before he built the Ka'bah. In the Deluge the Holy House was destroyed, but Abraham was directed to

---

[1] I Cor. 3:10,11.

[2] I Pet. 2:5.

[3] Eph. 2:20,21.

[4] *Sura* 3:90.

rebuild it, and on digging beneath the surface of its site he discovered the original foundation, and the Ka'bah was newly built upon that.

According to Muhammadan traditions, it was while Hagar was near the site of the Holy House, with her famishing son Ishmael, that a spring of water gushed forth with its life-giving stream from beneath that holy site. And that spring is the well Zemzem, or Zamzam, whose waters are deemed sacred and life-giving today.

Mount Arafat, a holy hill near Meccah, is another place of pilgrimage, and its sacredness dates from even an earlier day than the laying of the first foundation of the Holy House at Meccah by Adam. When our first parents were cast out of their heavenly paradise, Adam lighted in Ceylon, and Eve in Arabia. Seeking each other, they met on Mount Arafat, or the Mount of Recognition, and therefore that spot of their reunion and new covenanting is a place of pilgrimage and worship for the faithful of all the world at this time.[1] Adam is said to have built a *madaa*, a place of prayer, on Mount Arafat, before he built the Ka'bah.[2] The religion of Islam thus teaches its subjects to worship at the earliest threshold laid by our first parents in their primal covenanting, and all other religions recognize the importance of a similar idea.

---

[1] See Sale's *Koran*, "Preliminary Discourse," Sect.IV.; Burton's *Pilgrimage to El-medinah and Meccah*, III., 149-222, Hughes' *Dictionary of Islam*, s.vv. "Abraja,." "Ada,." "Arafat," "Hagar," "Ishmael.""Ka'bah," "Masjidu'l-Haram," "amzam;" Springer's *Life of Mohammad*, pp.46-62; Muir's *Mohamet and Islam*, pp.12-17,215-219.

[2] Burton's *Pilgrimage*, III., 260.

III.

SACRED BOUNDARY LINE.

1. FROM TEMPLE TO DOMAIN.

Man's first dwelling-place was the cave, or the tent, or the hut, in which he made a home with his family. The threshold and hearth of that dwelling-place was the boundary of his earthly possessions. It was the sacred border or limit of the portion of the earth's surface over which he claimed control, and where he and his were under the special protection of the deity with whom he was in covenant. Therefore the threshold hearth was hallowed as a place of covenant worship.

As families were formed into tribes and communities, they came to have a common ruler or priest, and his dwelling-place was counted by all as the common center of covenant with their common deity; and when they would worship that deity there, they worshiped at the threshold altar of his sanctuary. So it was that the threshold was the place of the hearth-fire and altar, in both house and temple.

When man acquired property rights beyond his dwelling-place, and communities and peoples gained control over portions of country more or less extensive, the boundary limits of their possessions were extended, but were no less real and positive than before. The protecting deity of the region thus bounded was recognized as having sway in that domain; and those who were dwellers there were in covenant relations with him. Therefore it was that the boundary line of such domain was deemed its threshold, and as such was held sacred as a place of worship and of sacrifice.

2. LOCAL LANDMARKS.

A private landmark was a sacred boundary, and was a threshold altar for its possessor. To remove or to disregard such a local threshold, was an offense not only against its owner, but against the deity in whose name it had been set up.

Among the earliest remains from unearthed Babylonia are local landmarks, or threshold boundary stones, inscribed, severally, with a dedication and an appeal to the deity honored by him who erected the stone. These local landmarks were ordinarily in the form of a phallus; as phallic forms were numerous under Babylonian temple thresholds. Among the records of those peoples are writings, showing the importance attached to such threshold stones, in the contracts accompanying their setting up, and in the sacred ceremonies on that occasion.

Illustrations of the importance attached by the ancient Babylonians to a boundary stone, or threshold landmark, are found in the records of the imprecations inscribed on these phallic pillars, as directed against the violator of their sacredness.[1]   For example, a Babylonian, Sir-usur ["O snake-god protect"], a descendant of the house of Habban, presented a valuable tract of land to his daughter on her betrothal to Tâbashâp-Marduk. The withering curse inscribed on the conventional boundary-stone pillar is as follows:

"For all future time: Whosoever, of the brothers, sons, family, relatives, descendants, servants purchased or house-born, of the house of Habban, be he a prefect, or an overseer, or anybody else, shall rise and stand up to take this field away, or to remove this boundary stone, and causes this field to be presented to a god, or sends someone to take it away [for the state], or brings it into his own possession; who changes the area, the limit, or the boundary stone, divides it into pieces, or takes a piece from it, saying, 'The field and *mulugi*[2] have not been presented;' or who on account of the dire curse [written] on this boundary stone, sends a fool, a deaf man, a blind man, a reckless man, an enemy, an alien, an ignorant man, and causes this inscribed stone to be removed, throws it into the water, hides it in the earth, crushes it with a stone, burns it with fire, effaces it and writes something else on it, or puts it into a place where nobody can see it,—upon this man may the great gods Anu, Bêl, Ea, and Nusku, look wrathfully, uproot his foundation, and destroy his offspring. May Marduk, the great lord,

---

[1]   See, for example, Rawlinson's *Cuneiform Inscriptions of Western Asia,* III., 41-43; IV., 41; Hilprecht's *Freibrief Nebukadnezar's,* I., col. II., 26-60; *Beitraege Zur Assyriologie.* II., 165-203, 258ff.

[2]   An unknown product of the field.

cause him to carry dropsy as an ever-entangling net; may Shamash the judge, greatest of heaven and earth, decide all his lawsuits, standing relentlessly against him; may Sin, the light dwelling in the brilliant heavens, cover him with leprosy as a garment; like a wild ass may he lie down at the wall surrounding his city; may Ishtar, mistress of heaven and earth, lead him into evil daily before the god and the king; may Ninib, born in the temple Ekura, the sublime son of Bêl, uproot his area, his limit, and his boundary stone; may Gula, the great physician, consort of the god Ninib, put never-ceasing poison into his body till he urinates blood and pus like water; may Rammân, first of heaven and earth, the strong son of the god Anu, inundate his field, and destroy the corn, that thorns may shoot up, and may his feet tread down vegetation and pasturage; may Nabû, the sublime messenger, bring want and famine upon him, and whatsoever he desires for the hole of his mouth may he not obtain; and may the great gods, as many names as are mentioned on this inscribed stone, curse him with a dire curse that cannot be removed, and destroy his seed for ever and ever."[1]

Prominence is given, in the ancient laws of India, to the manner in which disputed boundaries between villages, and between land owners, shall be settled; and it is made evident that a peculiar sacredness attaches to these landmarks. The king was to decide the dispute, after hearing testimony

[1] From the Michaux Stone, columns II.-IV. in Rawlinson's *Cuneiform Inscriptions of Western Asia*, I., pl.70; translated for this work by Prof. Dr. H.V. Hilprecht. See illustrations in Maspero's *Dawn of Civilization*, pp. 762, 763. See Sayce's *Religion of the Ancient Babylonians*, p. 308.

and examining evidence. Trees, and mounds, or heaps of earth, were preferred as landmarks; and tanks, wells, cisterns, and fountains, as also temples, were desired on boundary lines.[1]

Emphasis was laid on the sacredness of the local landmark, in the laws of the Hebrews; and a curse was pronounced against him who dared remove this threshold altar. "Thou shalt not remove thy neighbor's landmark, which they of old time have set, in thine inheritance which thou shalt inherit, in the land that the Lord thy God giveth thee," was an injunction in the fundamental law of the Promised Land.[2] And it passed into a proverb of duty: "Remove not the ancient landmark, which thy fathers have set."[3] It was a reproach to a people that there were those among them who would "remove the landmarks" and disregard sacred property rights.[4] And among the curses which were to be spoken from the summit of Ebal, when Israel took possession of Canaan, was this: "Cursed be he that removeth his neighbor's landmark. And," it was added, "all the people shall say, Amen."[5]

Abraham and Abimelech found that their followers were quarreling over the boundary line between their respective domains on the borders of the Negeb. Abraham

---

[1] Buhler's 'Laws of Manu," in *Sacred Books of the East*, XXV., 298, 301.

[2] Deut. 19:14 .

[3] Prov. 22:28; 23:10.

[4] Job 24:2.

[5] Deut. 27:17.

claimed the well at Beersheba as his by right, but the servants of Abimelech forcibly took possession off it. So the two chieftains met and agreed upon a border line, and made a covenant with accompanying sacrifices. "And Abraham planted a tamarisk tree in Beersheba" as his border landmark, "and called there on the name of the Lord, the Everlasting God."[1] Border landmarks were in the form of a pillar, a tree, a heap, or a stele, in Oriental countries generally.

When Jacob and Laban agreed to part in peace after their stormy meeting in Gilead, they set up a heap of stones and a stone pillar as a monument of witness of their mutual covenant, and as a landmark of their agreed territorial boundary. This memorial of their covenant was called "Galeed," or "Witness Heap," and "Mizpah," or "Watch Tower." "And Laban said to Jacob, Behold this heap, and behold the pillar, which I have set betwixt me and thee. This heap be a witness, and the pillar be witness, that I will not pass over this heap to thee, and that thou shalt not pass over this heap and this pillar unto me, for harm. The God of Abraham, and the God of Nahor, the God [or, gods] of their father, judge betwixt us."[2] The new boundary mark was a token of a sacred covenant.

In classic literature and customs the sacred boundary landmark is prominent as devoted to, or as representing, various deities, at different times. Zeus and Hermes among the Greeks; Jupiter, Mercury, Silvanus, and Terminus,

---

[1] Gen. 21:22-33.

[2] Gen. 31:43-53.

among the Romans, are sometimes interchangeably referred to in this connection. The legends and symbols employed seem to indicate that life and its transmission took their start at the threshold boundary, and therefore a pillar or a phallus marked every new beginning along a road or at a territorial boundary.

An image of Zeus, or Jupiter, was sometimes employed as a boundary landmark, and an image of Hermes, or Mercury, was at the starting-point of a road, and again at various points along the road. Zeus, or Jupiter, was chief of gods as the arbiter of life. Hermes, or Mercury, was earliest known as the fertilizing god of earth, and hence was the promoter of all forms of life, as guardian of flocks, fish, fields and fruits. He also guarded those who went out from the threshold. Sacrifices were offered to him by Athenian generals as they started on their expeditions. He was even spoken of as the inventor of sacrifices and the promoter of commerce and of enrichment.[1]

Of Terminus, Ovid says: "When the night shall have passed away [and the threshold of a new day is to be crossed], let the god who by his landmark divides the fields be worshiped with the accustomed honors. Terminus,[2]

---

[1] See Smith's *Classical Dictionary*, and Keightley's *Class. Dict.*, s.vv. "Hermes," "Jupiter," "Mercury," "Silvanus," "Terminus." "Zeus." Comp. Stengel's *Die griechischen Sacralaterthum*, in Iwan V. Muller's *Handbuch Der Klassischen Alterthumswissenschaft*, V., part 3, p.13; K. F. Hermann's *Lehrbuch Der Gottesdienstlichen Alterthumer Der Griechen*, pp. 73, 108, note 2.

[2] This god was represented by a stone or a stump, and not with human features." This would seem to have been a rude phallic form.

whether thou art a stone, or whether a stock sunk deep in the field by the ancients, yet even in this form thou dost possess divinity."[1] This symbol of Terminus was regularly "sprinkled with the blood of a slain lamb," in recognition of its sacredness.

It is said that Numa, the second king of Rome, who was revered by the Romans as the author of their whole system of religious worship, directed that everyone should mark the boundaries of his landed property by stones consecrated to Jupiter, and that yearly sacrifices should be offered at these boundary stones, at the festival of the Terminalia.[2] At this festival the two owners of adjacent property crowned the statue or stone pillar with garlands, and raised a rude altar, on which they offered up corn, honeycomb, and wine, and sacrificed a lamb or a sucking pig, with accompanying praises to the god.[3]

Silvanus also was a god of the boundary. He was represented by a tree grove, as Terminus was by a pillar, and offerings of fruit, grain, and milk, and of pigs, were made to him. When he would be guarded against as a source of evil in a home, the protectors of the inmates would perform certain ceremonies at the threshold of the house.

A tree, and sometimes a grove, was the sacred landmark of a village boundary in primitive lands. Such trees and groves are still to be found in Equatorial Africa. Describing some of these in Zinga and its vicinity, Stanley

---

[1] Ovid's *Fasti,* Bk. II., vs. 641ff.

[2] Smith's *Classical Dictionary*, s.vv. "Numa," "Terminus."

[3] Smith's *Dict. Of Greek and Rom. Antiq*., s.v."Terminalia."

expresses surprise that they have so long remained un-touched in "a country left to the haphazard care of patriar-chal chiefs ignorant of written laws."[1] But reverence for a threshold landmark seems to be in the very nature of a primitive people, as truly as any primitive sentiment; and sentiment is in itself a dominant law.

At the boundary line between two villages in Samoa, in olden time, there were two stones said to have been two living beings. When any quarrel arose, those engaged in it were told, "Go and settle it at the stones;" and they went to those boundary line stones and fought out their contest.[2]

Trees and stone pillars are still known as boundary landmarks between parishes and townships in Europe and America, as in Asia, Africa, and Polynesia in more primitive days; and their importance is recognized as peculiar, even if not always absolutely sacred. The annual custom of "beating the bounds" of a parish by the parish authorities survives in some parts of England today. A procession makes the circuit of the parish boundary, under the care of a "select vestryman," or other parish official, halting at every landmark to identify it and carefully to observe its location.

In former times it was customary to take the boys of the parish on this round, and beat them at every landmark, in order to impress upon their memories its precise position. More recently the boys are permitted to carry willow wands peeled white, and with these to beat the landmarks. The

---

[1] Stanley's *Congo*, I., 315-317.

[2] Turner's *Samoa*, p. 45f.

later plan is certainly more satisfactory to the boys, and it is quite as likely to impress their memories. Formerly this ceremony was accompanied by religious services, in which the clergyman invoked curses on him who "transgresseth the bounds and doles of his neighbor," and blessings on him who regarded the landmarks.[1]

It has been suggested that this fixing and honoring of the landmarks by an annual festival goes back to the Roman Terminalia, in the days of Numa, but there is reason to believe that it was far earlier than that. There are traces of it in primitive times, among various primitive peoples.

In Russia, the Cossacks long had a custom somewhat like this, in the case of a disputed boundary line. When the boundary had been formally determined, all the boys of the two continguous stanitsas, or land divisions, were collected, and driven by the people along the frontier line. "At each landmark a number of boys were soundly whipped and allowed to run home," in order that in later years they might be able to testify as to the spot where that landmark stood. In cases where the boys' memory failed to be accurate, an arbiter was chosen from the older inhabitants, and sworn to act honestly to the best of his knowledge and his decision was accepted as final.[2]

A similar custom of beating the bounds under a "selectman" of the town has existed in portions of New England until recently, and perhaps it has not yet died out there.

---

[1] See "Beating the Bounds," in Chambers' *Edinburgh Journal* for July 23, 1853, pp. 49-52; also *American Architect*, Vol .X., No. 293, p. 64f.

[2] Wallace's *Russia*, p. 306f.

Thus Ralph Waldo Emerson speaks of the selectmen of Concord perambulating the bounds of its township "once in five years," up to 1858.[1] Is there not a survival of this old custom in the habit of striking a child on his birthday as many blows as he has passed years, when he comes to the threshold of another year of his life?

Mile-posts would seem to have been originally land-marks separating the public way from private lands, being placed at regular distances along the road for convenience of measurement and locating. They marked the threshold of the "king's highway" to and from his capital in the Roman empire, as trees marked the border-lines of the principal roads in Greece.

3. NATIONAL BORDERS.

Stone pillars marking the exact boundaries of states or nations, whether settled by a joint commission or by a con-queror's fiat, are not a modern invention, although they are in use today. They are of old time, and of primitive ages. And these boundaries of a country are by their very nature its thresholds.

In Babylonia, the name of Nebuchadrezzar meant literally, "Nebo protect the boundary!" The theshold of the empire was sacred; and the deity, with whom the Babyloni-an king was in covenant, was the protector of that boundary, and of those who dwelt within it. From the earliest times onward an Oriental sovereign would set up a pillar, or

---

[1] Cited in Thompson's *Elements of Political Economy,* p. 110.

pillars, or stele, at the extreme limits of his newly extended dominion, as the outer threshold or doorway of his empire.

From Tiglath-Pileser I. to Esarhaddon, from about 1100 B.C. to 669 B.C., the great Assyrian kings tell us, in their inscriptions, that whenever they restored an old boundary of their predecessors that had been lost to them, or extended their boundary beyond its former limits, they had set up a large stele bearing their image at this threshold of their empire.[1] Frequently these stele doorways,[2] with the king represented on the threshold, had inscriptions on them giving the story of the new conquests, with an ascription of honor to the covenant god by whose power they had been wrought. Prominent mountain peaks, sources of rivers, the temples or market-places of conquered cities, the banks of lakes, or the shores of the sea, are chosen as conspicuous places for such steles. National boundary marks of this character are still to be seen on the rocks of Nahr-el-Kelb, above Beyroot, on the shores of the Mediterranean, and at the sources of the Tigris and the Euphrates.[3]

Ashurnâsirapli (king of Assyria, 885-860 B.C.) tells of such a new boundary mark set up by him at the farthest point of his conquests, "whither nobody of my royal ancestors had advanced . . . At that time I made a picture [a stele] of my person. The glory of my power I wrote upon it. On the mountain Eki, in the city Ashurnâsirapli [named

---

[1] Schrader's *Keilinschriftliche Bibliothek*, I., 63, 69, 87, 99, 109, 131, 133, 135, 141, 143, 147, 155, 159, 161, 165, 167, 169, 181; II.,19, 35, 54, 89.

[2] See pp. 105-108, supra.

[3] See for example, Schrader's *Keilinschriftliche Bibliothek*, I., 69.

after the king], at a spring I set it up."[1]

A similar custom would seem to have prevailed with the rulers of ancient Egypt. Sneferu, a king of the fourth dynasty, greatest among the very early names of the Old Empire (say, about 4000 B.C.), went down as a conqueror into the Peninsula of Sinai, and left there inscribed a mammoth figure of himself, on the granite hills above the famous copper and turquoise mines of Wady Magharah. He is styled in the accompanying inscription the "vanquisher of a foreign people."[2]

As early as the twelfth dynasty of ancient Egypt, before the days of Abraham, stone thresholds marked the upper border of that mighty empire. "Two huge pillars of stone, covered with long inscriptions, served formerly as boundary marks between the Egyptian empire and the negro-land called Heh."[3] King Usurtasen III., who set up these landmarks, says in an inscription on the second of them: "Every one of my sons who maintains this boundary which I have fixed, he shall be called my son who was born of me. My son is like the protector of his father (that is Horus), like the preserver of the boundary of his father (that is Osiris.) But if he abandons it, so that he does not fight upon it, he is not my son, he is not then born of me. I have caused my own image to be set up, on this boundary which I have fixed, not that ye may (only) worship it (the image of the

---

[1] Rawlinson's *Inscriptions of Western Asia*, I., 17-26, col. I, lines 63-69.

[2] Brugsch's *Egypt under the Pharaohs*, I., 8f.; Villiers Stuart's *Nile Gleanings*, Pl. xlv., p. 276.

[3] Brugsch's *Egypt under the Pharaohs*, I., 182f.

founder), but that ye may fight upon it."

On the oldest map in the world, a map of the gold districts in Nubia, in the nineteenth dynasty of Egypt, there is a mentioning of the "memorial stone of King Mineptah I. Seti I" And that memorial stone, of this new threshold of domain, marked the boundary line of empire in that direction.[1]

Rameses II, had it recorded on the walls of the rock grotto of Bayt-el-Walli concerning his threshold extensions: "The deeds of victory are inscribed a hundred thousand times on the glorious Persea. As the chastiser of the foreigners, *who has placed his boundary-marks according to his pleasure* in the land of the Ruthennu, he is in truth the son of Ra, and his very image."[2]

On the eastern border of Lower Egypt, the main passage way from the Delta into Arabia, the great gateway of the empire toward the north and the east, is still known as *El Gisr*, or "The Threshold."[3] This point is near Lake Timsah, on the line of the modern Suez Canal.

In ancient Greece, Theseus "set up a pillar," as a threshold stone between Peloponnesus and Attica,—then called Ionia, —"writing upon it an epigram in two trimeters, bounding the land. Of these [inscriptions] the one toward the east side said, 'This is not Pelopennesus, but Ionia,' and

---

[1] Brugsch's *Egypt under the Pharaohs*, II., 81f.

[2] Ibid., II., 78f.

[3] Trumbull's *Kadesh-barnea*, p. 341, note.

that toward the west, 'This is not Pelopennesus, but Ionia.'"[1]

Even the term, the "Pillars of Hercules," as the boundaries of the Grecian empire and the then known world, is an indication of this idea in the classic age, as well as in the primitive mind. Calpë and Abyla were the door-posts of the great outer passage way, and the threshold between those pillars was founded upon the seas, and established upon the floods.[2]

As showing that the term "threshold" is not applied to these boundary stones merely by accommodation, it is sufficient to quote from Justinian in the case. He declares specifically that "as the threshold makes a certain boundary in a house, so also the ancients designed that the boundary of the empire should be its threshold; hence it is called the 'threshold', as if it were a certain bound and term."[3] Speaking of one who has been in foreign captivity, and who desires a resumption, or a restoration, of his civil rights, on his coming back to his country, Justinian says that such a return "is called *postliminium* [a recrossing of the threshold], because at that same threshold the thing which he has lost is restored to him."[4]

When the old Portuguese navigators started out on their voyages of discovery, they were accustomed to take with them stone pillars to set up in a prominent place at the

---

[1] Plutarch's *Lives,* Theseus, 25.

[2] Psa. 24:2

[3] Justinian, *Inst.*, Lib. I., 12, 5.

[4] *Ibid.*

farthest limits of their newly claimed territory as the national door-posts or threshold in that direction. Such a pillar was erected at the mouth of the Congo River, at the time of its discovery by Diego Cào, or Cam, in 1484-85. On this account, the river was known for a time as the "Rio de Padrào," or "Pillar River."[1] It might, indeed, have been called the "River of the Threshold."

This custom of setting up stone pillars as boundary marks along the borders of countries, nations, and states has been continued down to the present day. Such landmarks are still to be seen along the borders of the great divisions of Europe and they are on the lines of the several states of the United States of America. The line between the English grants in America, originally made to the Duke of York and to Lord Baltimore, was, after much dispute, run by two English surveyors, Charles Mason and Jeremiah Dixon, in 1763-67, and marked by stone pillars at intervals of five miles. This was generally known as "Mason and Dixon's line;" it separated Pennsylvania from Delaware, Maryland and Virginia, and was the dividing line between the free and the slave states before the Civil War of 1861-65. One of those early stone landmarks on that line is still to be seen near Oxford, in Chester County, Pennsylvania, as an illustration of a practice beginning in Babylonia as far back as 4000 B.C., and continued in America down to A.D. 1895.[2]

European titles of rank bear traces of the importance

---

[1] Stanley's *Congo*, I., I-II.

[2] See *Penn. Mag of Hist. And Biog.*, VI., 412-434

formerly attached to national boundary lines and their preservation. The old German title of "markgraf," the "graf" or count or warden of the marches, designated a representative or servant of the king who was in charge of the "marches," or "marks," or "border lines" which guarded the thresholds of the empire in different directions. It was under "Henry the Fowler," early in the tenth century that this title, as a title, first gained prominence. Afterwards it became hereditary, and hence have come the innumerable margraves, marquises and such like of modern times.[1]

"Letters of marque" were letters of commission, or permission, granted by the government to individuals, in time of war, to pass over the boundary mark, or national threshold, for purposes of seizure or reprisal. And a "marquee" is primarily a tent over, or before, the threshold of a military commander's tent.

4. BORDER SACRIFICES

An altar would have no meaning unless sacrifices were offered at it. If, therefore, the boundary threshold of an empire were an altar for that empire, sacrifices would surely be offered there; and the records of history and the customs of old times and later, show this to have been the case.

Sacrifices were offered at the new boundary of an empire, by ancient Assyrian and Egyptian kings, when they set up a pillar, or stele, at the freshly acquired threshold in

---

[1] Caryle's *History of Frederick, II.,* I., 71-74.

that direction. Thus, for example, Ashurnâsirapli (king of Assyria 885-860 B.C.), telling of his far-reaching conquests, says that he marched with his armies to the slopes of the Lebanon, and to the sea of the Westland, and that at the mountains of Ammanus he made and set up a stele of victory, and offered sacrifices unto his gods.[1]

At the Egyptian boundary line in the Sinaitic Peninsula, there was a temple with its sacrifices to "the sublime Hathor, queen of heaven and earth and the dark depths below, whom the Egyptians worshiped as the protectress of the land of mafkat." There were other temples with their sacrifices at that point."[2] On the southern boundary of Egypt, in the gold district of Nubia, there was the "temple of Amon in the holy mountain," where threshold sacrifices were offered.[3]

One of the most ancient of Chinese classics is the Shih King. Its age is not known, but it is certain that it was a classic in the days of Confucius, five centuries before the Christian era. This work contains frequent references to sacrifices at the border altars, or the altars of the boundary. There were public sacrifices at the "border altar " in the beginning of every new year; and again when a ruler crossed his border line, on a warlike mission.[4]

---

[1] Rawlinson's *Inscriptions of Western Asia*. I., 17-26. Col III., II. 84-89.

[2] Brugseh's *Egypt Under the Pharaohs*, I., 81.

[3] Brugseh's *Egypt under the Pharaohs*, II., 82.

[4] "The Shih King" in *Sacred Books of the East*. III., 343, 392, note, 420, 422 note.

When, in ancient times, a Chinese emperor passed over
the outer threshold of his empire, he offered a sacrifice of a
dog, by running over it with the wheels of his chariot. This
is supposed to have been a propitiatory offering to the dog-
shaped guardians of the roadway threshold, known also
among, the Indo-Aryans and the Assyro-Babylonians.[1]

From what is known of modern customs in this line,
and from occasional historical references to the matter, it
would seem that, where there were no gateways, or
double columns to stand for door-posts, or doorway stele, it
was the practice to divide or separate the animals offered in
sacrifice, so as to make a passageway between them, as
through a door or gate, and to pour out the blood of the
victims on the earth between the two portions, so that the
offerer or the one welcomed, might pass over, or step
across, that blood, as in a threshold covenant.

It has already been shown that when General Grant
came to the border line of Assioot, in upper Egypt, as he
landed from his Nile boat, a bullock was sacrificed in
covenant welcome, its head being put on one side of the
gangland, and its body on the other; while its blood was
between the two, so that it should be stepped over in the act
of landing.[2] And every year, when the great Hajj procession
returns from Meccah to Syria, it is welcomed by just such
sacrifices as this. Sheep and oxen are sacrificed before the
caravan, their blood being poured out in the middle of the

---

[1] Lacouperie's *Western Origin of the Early Chinese Civilization*, pp. 79,
81.

[2] See page 7 f., *ante*.

road, and their bodies being divided and placed on either side of the way. Then those who approach by this "new and living way,"[1] on the boundary line of their country, renew their covenant with those within, by passing over the blood.[2]

There seems to be a reference to such a mode of boundary sacrifices, in the description of the Lord's covenant welcome to Abraham, on the border of the land promised to him for a possession.[3] Abraham was near the southern boundary of Canaan. He had the promise of the Lord, that he and his seed should possess that land; but as yet he was childless, and he had no control over any portion of the land. He naturally desired some tangible assurance, in accordance with the customs of mankind that the Lord's promises to him would be made good. Therefore when the Lord said to him, "I am the Lord that brought thee out of Ur of the Chaldees, to give thee this land to inherit it," Abraham replied with the question, "O Lord God, whereby shall I know that I shall inherit it?"

"And he took him all these and divided them in the midst, and had each half over against the other: but the birds divided he not." The blood of the victims was doubtless poured out on the earth where they were sacrificed, midway between the pieces of the divided portions, as is the present custom.

"And it came to pass, that when the sun went down and it was dark, behold a smoking furnace [or brazier, or

---

[1] Heb 10:20

[2] I have this on testimony of those who have often witnessed it.

[3] See Gen. 15:1-21.

censer], and a flaming torch [a fire and a light as a symbol of the Divine presence] that passed [covenant-crossed the blood on the threshold] between these pieces." And the record adds: In that day the LORD made a covenant [a border-altar covenant] with Abram, saying, Unto thy seed have I given this land, from the river of Egypt unto the great river, the river Euphrates: the Kenite, and the Kenizzite, and the Kadmonite, And the Hittite, and the Perizzite, and the Rephaim, And the Amorite, and the Canaanite, and the Girgashite, and the Jebusite."

Thus Abram was assured that the Lord had covenanted to protect his boundaries; as Nebuchadrezzar long afterward desired that his god Nebo would protect his empire boundary or threshold. As to the fact of boundary sacrifices in these lands and elsewhere, in those days and earlier, there would seem to be no room for question.

It is not to be expected that border sacrifices would at all times, and in all places, be just alike; but a common primitive symbolism would be likely to show itself in them all. In Persia, these sacrifices are still common, when one is to be received with honors at the border of a new territory or jurisdiction.[1] Morier, describing his journey through Persia, in the early part of this century, speaks of the first entrance of a new ruler into the territory he was to govern. "The khan, with all his attendants, accompanied us about two miles. He was preparing to enter Bushire, his new government with all splendor. From the town to the swamps [from the territorial border to the border of the capital] were erected stages on which bullocks were to be sacrificed, and

---

[1] On this point I am assured by missionaries and other dwellers in Persia.

from which their heads were to be thrown under his horse's feet as he advanced; a ceremony, indeed, appropriated to princes alone, and to them only on particular occasions.[1]

On another occasion, when the British envoy approached Kauzeroon, on a visit of ceremony, he was welcomed at the threshold of the town by a corresponding ceremony. "A bottle which contained sugar candy was broken under the feet of the envoy's horse, a ceremony never practiced in Persia to any but to royal personages."[2]

Again, when the Shah of Persia was to enter Teheran, he was received outside of the walls, by prominent officials, with much ceremony. As he approached the gates, "oxen and sheep in great numbers were sacrificed just as he passed, and their heads thrown under his horse's feet." And "glass vases filled with sugar were broken before him." On this occasion the Shah frequently looked at a watch, "anxious that he should enter the gates exactly at the time prescribed by the astrologers" for his crossing the threshold.[3]

More recently, Layard has testified to the prevalence of such customs. Speaking of his reception among the Yezidis, he tells of his approach to the village of Guzelder, and of his welcome there: "The head of the village of Guzelder, with the principal inhabitants, had come to invite me to eat bread in his house, and we followed him. . .Before we reached Guzelder, the procession had swollen to many

---

[1] Morier's *Journey to Constantinople*, p. 75

[2] *Ibid*, p. 84f. See, also, Morier's *Second Journey through Persia*, p. 93f.

[3] Morier's *Second Journey through Persia*, p. 387f.

hundreds . . . . As I approached, sheep were brought into the road and slain before my horse's feet, and as we entered the yard of Akko's house the women and men joined in the loud and piercing '*tahlel*' "[1]

Again, as Layard entered the village of Redwan, he was similarly welcomed. "I alighted," he says, "amidst the din of music and the '*tahlel*' at the house of Nazi, the chief of the whole Yezidi district; two sheep being slain before me as I took my feet from the stirrups."[2]

When some twenty years ago, a European prince visited the Mt. Lebanon region,[3] a generous host killed a valuable cow on the road by which the prince must come into his region. The royal visitor and his retinue were requested to step over, not upon, the blood of the slaughtered cow, at the threshold of that host's domain.

On the occasion of a caravan starting out from the boundary line of a country in the East, there are border sacrifices offered, even in recent times. Thus Burckhardt tells of this ceremony, when he went from Egypt to Nubia.

The various traders going with this caravan assembled at the starting point, having their goods with them. "At noon the camels were watered, and knelt down by the side of their respective loads. Just before the lading commenced, the Arabade women appeared with earth vessels in their hands, filled with burning coals. They set them before the

---

[1]   Layard's Ninevah and Babylon (Am. Ed), p. 35f.

[2]   *Ibid.* p. 37

[3]   My informant, an eyewitness of this incident, was not sure whether it was a Prussian, an Austrian, or a Russian prince.

several loads, and threw salt upon them." It has already been shown that salt stands for blood, in the minds of primitive peoples. "At the rising of the bluish flame produced by the burning of the salt, they exclaimed, 'May you be blessed in going and in coming!'"[1] And this sacrifice was supposed to secure safety against evil spirits encountered in crossing the boundary line.

Thus it would seem that, from the beginning, on the national threshold, as on the threshold of the temple and of the home, sacrifices were set up in recognition of a peculiar sacredness of the border line,—which is in itself a foundation and a limit. These boundary marks were commonly a pillar or a tree, in apparent symbolism of a fructifying or a fruit-bearing agency, of the transmission or the continuance of life. And the establishment and protection of these boundary marks was deemed well pleasing to God, or to the gods, and in the nature of a holy covenant service.

[1] Burckhardt's *Travels in Nubia*, p. 157.

IV.

ORIGIN OF THE RITE

1. A NATURAL QUESTION

A question that forces itself on the mind, in connection with the study of a world-wide primitive rite like this of the Threshold Covenant, is, What was its origin? How came it to pass, that primitive peoples, in all parts of the world, were brought to attach such exceptionally sacred significance to the threshold of a hut, or tent, or cave, or house; of a palace or temple; of a domain, local or national; and to count its crossing by blood a form of holy covenanting between the parties engaged in it, and the deity invoked in the ceremony? This question goes back to the origin of religious rites among human beings, and its answer must, in order to commend itself to all, be in accordance with the natural outgrowths and the abnormal perversions of religious rites, in the main line of human development all the world over.

However simple and elemental were man's earliest religious ideas, they must have been from the beginning pure and uplifting, or they would not have been religious. Nothing impure or debasing in itself would have raised man's thoughts Godward, even though man might subsequently come to degrade his best conceptions of God and his worship. Hence the answer to this question must include only such facts as

175

were capable of being viewed reverently by primitive man, as worthy of God's creatures in the loving service and worship of God.

2. AN ANSWER BY INDUCTION

This threshold rite clearly goes back to the beginning of family life. The facts already presented are proof of this. The rite includes the proffer of blood at the foundation of the family as a family. It is a part of the marriage ceremonial among primitive peoples. It is also the means by which one is adopted from without into a family's circle or group. It marks every stage of the progress of family life, from one party to a community and to an empire, in its civil and religious relations. It is a form of covenanting between it participants, and between them and God; an thus it has sanctity as a religious rite.

A fair induction from these recognized facts, in their sweep and significance, would seem to indicate, as the origin of this primitive rite, the covenant union between the first pair in their instituting of the family relation. When was the first covenant made between two human beings? When was the first outpouring of blood in loving sacrifice? By what act was the first appeal made to the Author and Source of life for power for the transmission of life, by two persons who thereby entered into covenant with each other and with him? The obvious answer to these questions is an answer to the question, What was the origin of the rite of the Threshold covenant?

Life and its transmission must have been a sacred mystery to the first thinkers about God and his human workers. Blood was early recognized as life, its outpouring as the pledge and gift of life, and its interchange as a life covenant between those who shared its substance. In view of this truth, a covenant union by blood that looked to the transmission of life must have been in itself, to a thoughtful and reverent person, as appeal to the Author of life to be a part to that covenant union, in order to give it efficiency.

When first a twain were made one in a covenant of blood, the threshold altar of the race was hallowed as place where the Author life met and blessed the loving union. And from this beginning there was the natural development of religious rites and ceremonies, in the family, in the temple, and in the domain, as shown alike in the history of the human race and in the main teachings of both the Old Testament and the New.

3. NO COVENANT WITHOUT BLOOD

Flowing blood is widely deemed essential to the covenant by which two are made one in the marriage relation. This is peculiarly the case among those primitive peoples where young maidens are guarded with jealous care, and are given in marriage at a very early age. In the thought of such peoples there is no binding covenant without blood, in the family relations.[1] And a bloody hand stamp on the cloth of testimony is the primitive certificate of the marriage covenant.

Facts in illustration of this truth are numerous in the

---

[1] The recognition of this truth is a reason for the infibulation of female children among primitive peoples. (See, for example, Captain J. S. King's "Notes on the Folk-Lore , and some Social Customs of the Western Somah Tribes," in the London *Folk-Lore Journal* VI., 124; also Dr. Remondino's *History of Circumcision,* p. 51.)

nuptial customs of Syria, Egypt, China, Dahomey, Liberia, Europe, Central America, Samoa, and other widely different regions. A few of these facts are given in the [Latin language] Appendix for the benefit of scientific students, in a language better suited than English for the presentation of such details.[1]

4. CONFIRMATION OF THIS VIEW

If the view presented here of the origin of this rite of the Threshold Covenant be correct, there will be found traces of the truth in the different religions of mankind. And this is the case, as shown in religious literatures, in history, and in primitive customs and beliefs.

The most ancient expression of the religious thought and feeling of the Aryan races is found in the Vedas and their accompanying literature. The Brahmanas, in this literature, deal with the sacrificial element in public and family worship, and with the rites and ceremonies pertaining to religion. In the description of the construction of the household altars and the high altars, there is abundant evidence that the woman is recognized as the primitive altar, and that the form of the woman is made the pattern of the altar form.

It is distinctly declared as to the shape of the altar, standing east and west, that it "should be broader on the west side, contracted on the middle, and broad again on the east side; for thus shaped they praise a woman: 'broad about the hips, somewhat narrower between the shoulders, and contracted in the middle [or about the waist].'" Again, it is

---

[1] Dr. Trumbull refers here to the nine pages of Latin Appendix which is not included in this edition.

said, in explanation, that "the altar (*vedi*, feminine) is female and the fire (*agni*, masculine) is male."[1] This identifying of the altar with the woman, of the offering with the man and covenanting, is repeatedly found in the Brahmanas.[2]

Even as far back as the Vedas themselves the term *yoni*, or doorway of physical life, is used as synonymous with altar.[3] And the production of sacred fire, for purposes of worship, by twisting a stick in softened wood, is described in the Rig-Vedas as a form of this covenant rite. These facts point to this origin of the threshold altar of covenant and sacrifice.

At present in India the most widely recognized visible aid in worship is the representation of the *linga* and the *yoni* combined. This symbol nominally stands for Siva; but that seems to be only because Saivism predominates in modern Hindoosim. The idea of this symbolic combination long antedates this prominence of Siva worship.[4]

A form of Booddist prayer in Tibet, said to be repeated more frequently than any other known among men, is the six-syllabled sentence, "*Om mani padme Hum;* —'Om! The Jewel

---

[1] See "Satapatha Brâhmana," 1. Kânda, 2 Adhyâya, 5 Brâhmana. 14-16, in *Sacred Books of the East,* XII., 62f.; also "Satapatha Brâhmana," III., 5, I. II. In *Sac. Bks. of East,* XXVI., 113.

[2] "Satapatha Brâhmana," 1. 3. 1, 18; I.,9, 2, 5-11, 21-24; II., 1, 4 in *Sac. Bks. of East,* 74, 257, 262, 277; also "Satapatha Brâhmana," III., 3, 1, 11; III., 8, 4.7-13 in *Sac. Bks. of East,* XXVI., 61, 211-214.

[3] See , II., 36.4; X., 18.7 Comp. "Satapatha Brâhmana," I., 7, 2, 14 in *Sac. Bks. of East,* XII., 194; also "Satapatha Brâhmana," IV., I, 2, 9,; IV., 1,3, 19,with note, in *Sac. Bks. of East,* XXVI*., 260,269. See, also, Hopkin's *Religions of India,* p. 490, and note.

[4] Compare Sir Monier Monier-William's *Brâhmanism and Hinduism,* pp. 33, 54f. 223 f. And Wilkin's *Hindu Mythology,* p. 233f.

in the Lotus! Hum!'" This prayer is simply a euphemism for the primitive Threshold Covenant, as here explained, with an ejaculatory invocation and ascription before and after it.[1] It seems of be a survival of the thought that here was the beginning of the religious rites, and that all covenant worship must continue in its spirit and power.

Every repetition of that prayer, by speech or by mechanism, is supposed to affect the progress of a soul in crossing the threshold of one of the stages of being in the universe. It is a help to new birth for some soul somewhere.

There would thus appear to be no room for doubt in this matter in the language and customs of the primitive Aryan peoples, and there are also confirmations of the idea among the Semites. A legend that has a place among the Jews and the Muhammadans, tells of a visit of Abraham to the home of Hagar and Ishmael in Arabia.[2] An Amalekite wife of Ishmael refused hospitality to Abraham, and in consequence Abraham

---

[1]   Sir Monier Monier-William's *Buddhism*, pp. 371-373. This writer, speaking of the prominence in India of the symbolism of the *linga* and the *yoni* combined, ascribes it to the theory of the two essences, "Spirit regarded as a male principle, and Matter, or the germ of the external world, regarded as a female." He says: "Without the union of the two no creation takes place. To any one imbued with these dualistic conceptions the *linga* and the *yoni* are suggestive of no improper ideas. They are either types of the two mysterious creative forces... or symbolic of one divine power delegating procreative energy to male and female organisms. They are mystical representatives, and perhaps the best impersonal representatives of the abstract expressions 'paternity' and 'maternity,' [and their conjunction in marital union]. (*Brâhmanism and Hinduism*, p. 224 f.)

[2]   This legend is found in *Pirqe de R. Eliezer*. Chap. XXX. The Hebrew words *saph* and *miphta*n are here employed for "threshold." It is also given in Macoundt's *Les Prairies d'Or*, chap 39, p. 94. Here the Arabic is *atabah*, for "threshold." See, also, Spenger's *Life of Mohammed*, p. 53f.

left a message to Ishmael to "change his threshold." This message Ishmael understood to mean the putting away of his wife and the taking of another, and he acted accordingly. In the Arabic "a wife" is one of the meanings of the term "threshold."[1]

And the term "gate," or "door," had among the rabbis a special application to the altar of family covenanting. Thus Buxtorf, in his definings of *"janua"* and *"ostium,"* says plainly: *"Apud rabbinos etiam est 'ostium ventris muliebris.'"* And he quotes the saying of a disappointed bridegroom: *"Ostium apertum inveni."*[2]

Among the early Babylonians and Egyptians, as among other primitive peoples, the twofold symbols of sex are counted the sacred emblem of life, and as such are borne by the gods of life, and by those who have the power of life and death from those gods. The circle and rod, or ring and bolt, conjoined, are in the right hand of the Babylonian sun-god Shamash:[3] as in the *ankh*, or *crux ansata*, they are in the right hand of every principal deity of ancient Egypt.[4] It is much the

---

[1] See Lane *Arabic-English Lexicon,* s.v. "Atabah;" and Dozy's *Supplement aux Dictionnaries Arabes,* s.v. "Atabah."

[2] Buxtorf's *Lex. Chald. Tal. et Rabb.,* s.v. "Pethakh." See, also, the Talmudic treatise *Nidda,* Mishna, § 2, 5.

[3] See, for example, illustration in Maspero's *Dawn of Civil.* P. 657; also Sayce's *Relig. Of Anc. Babyl.,* p. 285

[4] Wilkinson's *Ancient Egyptians,* III., 3, 8, 14, 18, 21, 22, 31, 36, 37, 40, 41, 45, 46, 60, 63, 66, 87, 100, 115, 118, 122, 129, 133, 135, 137, 146, 156, 158, 163, 170, 172, 175, 177, 180, etc.

same with the Phoenicians and others.[1]

In the innermost shrine of the most sacred Shinto temples of Japan, the circular mirror, and the straight dagger, with the same meaning as the circle and rod in Babylonia and Egypt and Phoenicia, are the only indications of the presence of deity; and the worshipers in those temples can come no farther than the threshold of the shrine containing these emblems.[2]

Wherever, among the primitive peoples in America, as elsewhere, the red hand is found as a symbol of covenant, and of life and strength through covenant, it would seem to point to this primal meaning of he hand stamp of blood at the doorway of life in a sacred covenant. There are indications in Central American sculptures of the sacredness attaching to the covenant rite between the first pair; and the combined symbols of sex are represented there as in the East.[3]

It is a well known fact that the public exhibit of the primitive Threshold Covenant, as here explained, has been continued as a mode of reverent worship among primitive peoples in the South Sea Islands, down to modern times. The testimony of Captain Cook, the famous navigator, is specific on this point.[4] It is also to be noted that in these islands the

---

[1] See Perrot and Chipiez's *Hist of Art in Phoenicia and Cyprus,* I., 80, 320. See, also, Layard's *Nineveh and its Remains,* II., 168-170 (Am.ed); and an article by Hommel in "Proceedings of the Society of Biblical Archaeology" for January, 1893.

[2] Hearn's *Glimpses of the Unfamiliar Japan,* II., 397, note; Lowell's *Occult Japan,* pp. 270-273.

[3] See Bancroft's *Native Races and Anti.,* III., 504-506.

[4] *Voyages of Capt. James Cook,* "First Voyage" at May 14, 1769. Also Voltaire's *Les Oreilles du Comte de Chesterfield,* Ch VI. See Appendix.

two supports of the altar, or table of sacrifice, are seeming symbols of the two sexes, similar to those used in the far East.[1]

All of the gathered facts concerning the Threshold Covenant in different lands and in different times, as presented in the foregoing pages, would seem to be in accordance with this view of he origin of the rite, as with no other that can be suggested. The main symbolism of both the Old and the New Testament also seem to indicate the same beginning.

[1] See Cook's *Voyage to Pacific Ocean*, volume of plates; also Ellis's *Poly. Res*, II., 217.

THE THRESHOLD COVENANT

V.

HEBREW *PASS-OVER*, OR *CROSS-OVER* SACRIFICE

I. NEW MEANING IN AN OLD RITE.

How the significance of the Hebrew Passover rite stands out in the light of this primitive custom! It is not that this rite had its origin in the days of the Hebrew exodus from Egypt, but that Jehovah then and there emphasized the meaning and sacredness of a rite already familiar to Orientals. In dealing with his chosen people, God did not invent a new rite or ceremonial at every stage of his progressive revelation to them; but he took a rite with which they were already familiar, and gave to it a new and deeper significance in its new use and relations.

Long before that day, a covenant welcome was given to a guest who was to become as one of the family, or to a bride or bridegroom in marriage, by the outpouring of blood on the threshold of the door, and by staining the doorway itself with the blood of the covenant. And now Jehovah announced that he was to visit Egypt on a designated night, and that those who would welcome him should prepare a threshold covenant, or a pass-over sacrifice, as a proof of that welcome; for where no such welcome was made ready for him by a family, he must count the household as his enemy.[1]

In announcing this desire for a welcoming sacrifice by the Hebrews, God spoke of it as "Jehovah's pass-over," as if the pass-over rite was a familiar one, which was now to be observed as a welcome to Jehovah.[2] Moses, in reporting the Lord's message to the Hebrews, did not speak of the proposed sacrifice as something of which they knew nothing until now, but he first said to them, "Draw out, and take you lambs according to your families, and kill the passover"—or the threshold cross-over;[3] and then he added details of special instruction for this new use of the old rite.

2. A WELCOME WITH BLOOD.

A lamb was the chosen sacrifice in the welcome to Jehovah. Each household, or family, was to take one lamb for this offering. No directions were given as to the place or manner of its sacrifice; for that seems to have been understood by all, because of the very term "pass-over," or threshold cross-over. This is implied, indeed, in the directions for the use of the blood when it was poured out: "Kill the passover," in the usual place; "and ye shall take a bunch of hyssop, and dip it in the blood that is at the *threshold* [Hebrew, *saph*], and strike the lintel and the two

---

[1] See Exod. 12:1-20.

[2] Exod. 12:11

[3] Exod. 12:21,27.

side posts with the blood that is at the *threshold*." [1]

In that welcome with blood there was covenant protection from Jehovah as he came into Egypt to execute judgment on his enemies. The Egyptians had already refused him allegiance, and put themselves in open defiance of his authority. They were now to be visited in judgment. [2] But in order to the distinguishing of the Lord's people from his enemies, the Hebrews were to prepare a blood welcome at their doorway, and the Lord would honor this welcome by covenanting with those who proffered it.

"And Moses said, Thus saith the Lord, About midnight will I go out into the midst of Egypt: and all the firstborn in the land of Egypt shall die, from the firstborn of Pharaoh that sitteth upon his throne, even unto the firstborn of the maidservant that is behind the mill; and all the firstborn of cattle . . . But against any of the children of Israel shall not a dog move his tongue, against man or beast; that ye may know how that the Lord doth put a difference between the Egyptians and Israel. [3]

In furtherance of this purpose, the Lord asked for the sacrifice of the threshold cross-over by the Hebrews: "For the Lord will pass through [the land] to smite the Egyptians; and when he seeth the blood upon the lintel, and on the two side posts [of the Hebrew homes], the Lord will pass over [cross-over or through] the door, and will not suffer the

---

[1] Exod. 12:22.

[2] Exod. 2:23-25; 3:7-10; 5:1,2; 6:1-7; 10:21-19.

[3] Exod. 11:4-7.

destroyer to come in unto your houses to smite you." [1]
Obviously the figure here employed is of a sovereign
accompanied by his executioner, a familiar figure in the
ancient East. When he comes to a house marked by tokens
of the welcoming covenant, the sovereign will
covenant-cross that threshold, and enter the home as a
guest, or as a member of the family; but where no such
preparation has been made for him, his executioner will
enter on his mission of judgment. [2]

3. BASON, OR THRESHOLD.

It is strange that the Hebrew word for "threshold"
(*saph*) in this narrative is translated "bason" in our English
Bible. It is because of this that the identity of the passover
sacrifice with the primitive Threshold Covenant is so
generally lost sight of. This word *saph* occurs many times
in the Old Testament text, and in nine cases out of ten it is
translated "threshold," or "door," or "door-post," or the
like. [3] It would seem that it should be so translated in this
instance.

In some cases where *Saph* is translated "bason," or

---

[1] Exod. 12:23.

[2] Compare Josh. 2:1-21; 6:16-25

[3] See, for example, Judg.19:27; I Kings 14:17; 2 Kings 12:9,13; 22:4;
23:4; 25:18; I Chron. 9:19, 11; 2 Chron. 3:7; 23:4; 34:9; Esther 2:21; 6:2;
Isa. 64; Jer. 35:4; 52:19,24; Ezek. 40:6,7; 41:16; 43:8; Amos 9:1; Zeph.
2:14; Zech. 12:2

"cup," the term "threshold" would be more appropriate, as when included in an enumeration of the temple furniture.[1] Bronze and silver thresholds were often mentioned in the furniture of Babylonian and Assyrian temples;[2] and they might well have had mention among the Hebrews. It is possible, however, that there was a cavity, as a blood receptacle, in the threshold of houses or temples where sacrifices were so frequent; and this would account for the use of the word *saph* as "bason," even where it referred to the threshold of the door.

The translators of the Septuagint, living in Egypt and familiar with the customs of that land, rendered *saph* by *thyra*, "doorway,"[3] in the story of the exodus. Jerome, with his understanding of Oriental life, gives *limen,* "threshold," for *saph*, at this point.[4] Philo Judaeus, out of his Egyptian Jewish experiences, describing the Jewish passover festival, speaks of it as "the feast *Disbateria,* which the Jews called *Paskha.*"[5] *"Disbateria"* are offerings before crossing a border,"[6] or threshold sacrifices. Rabbi Ishmael, a Talmudist, in explaining the passage descriptive of the institution of the passover in Egypt, says: "One dug a hole

---

[1]   See, for example, Jer.52:19.

[2]   See pp. 109-111, supra.

[3]   See *Septuagint*, in loco.

[4]   See *Vulgate*, in loco.

[5]   Philo's *Pera*, Mangey, 2:292.

[6]   Liddell and Scott's *Greek-English Lexicon*, s.v.

in the [earthen] threshold, and slaughtered into that," "for *saph* signifies here nothing else than threshold."[1]

A striking illustration of the error of translating *saph* "a bason" or "a cup," is shown in the rendering of Zechariah 12:1-3 in our English Bible. The Lord is there promising to protect the borders of Jerusalem against all besiegers. "Thus saith the Lord, which . . . layeth the foundation of the earth . . . Behold, I will make Jerusalem a *threshold* [or, boundary stone, Hebrew, *saph*] of reeling unto all the peoples round about . . . I will make Jerusalem a burdensome stone for all the peoples." The figure seems to be that of the besiegers staggering as they come against that foundation, or threshold stone, which the Lord has established. Yet *saph* is here translated "cup," and the passage thereby rendered meaningless.

There would seem, indeed, to be little room for doubt that *saph* should be translated "threshold" in the description of the passover sacrifice. In Assyrian, the word *sippu*, from the same root as the Hebrew *saph*, means only threshold, not bason or cup.[2]

4. PASS-OVER OR PASS-BY.

The common understanding of the term "passover," in connection with the Hebrew exodus from Egypt, is that it

---

[1] Cited in Levy's *Neuheb.Wörterb.*, s.v."Saph."

[2] This on authority of Prof. Dr. H. V. Hilprecht.

was, on the Lord's part, a passing by those homes where the doorways were blood-stained, without entering them. Yet this meaning is not justified by the term itself, nor by the significance of the primitive rite. Jehovah did not merely spare his people when he visited judgment on the Egyptians. He covenanted anew with them by passing over, or crossing over, the blood-stained threshold into their homes, while his messenger of death went into the houses of the Lord's enemies and claimed the first-born as belonging to Jehovah.[1]

This word *pesakh*, translated "passover," is a peculiar one. Its etymology and root meaning have been much in discussion. It is derived from the root *pasakh* "to cross over," a meaning which is still preserved in the Hebrew word *Tiphsakh*, the name of a city on the banks of the Euphrates,[2] the Hebrew equivalent of the classical Thapsacus.[3] *Tiphsakh* means "crossing," apparently so

---

[1] Among primitive peoples it was a common thought that the first fruits of life in any sphere belonged of right to God, or the gods. This was true of the fields, of the flocks and herds, and of the family. (See, for example, Frazer's *Golden Bough*, II., 63-78, 373-384; also W. Robertson Smith's *Religion of the Semites*, pp. 443-446.) As in Egypt particular gods were supposed to have power over men and beasts in special localities, the first-born belonged to them, and stood as representing their power and protection; yet Jehovah claimed to be Lord over all. And now, at the close of the contest between God and the gods, Jehovah took to himself out of the homes of his enemies the devoted first-born of man and of beast, in evidence of the truth that the gods of Egypt could not protect them.

[2] 1 Kings 4:24, "Tiphsah"

[3] See Gesenius' *Hebr. And Aram. Handworterbuch* (12th ed.), s.v. "Tiphsakh."

called from the ford of the Euphrates at that place.

Later Jewish traditions and customs point to the meaning of the original passover rite as a crossing over the threshold of the Hebrew homes by Jehovah, and not of his passing by his people in order to their sparing. A custom by which a Hebrew slave became one of the family in a Hebrew household, through having his ear bored with an awl at the door-post of the house, and thereby blood staining the doorway,[1] is connected with the passover rite by the rabbis. "The Deity said: The door and the side-posts were my witnesses in Egypt, in the hour when I passed-over the lintel and the two side-posts, and I said that to Me the children of Israel shall be slaves, and not slaves to slaves; I brought them out from bondage to freedom; and this man who goeth and taketh a lord to himself shall be bored through before these witnesses."[2]

According to Jewish traditions, it was on a passover night when Jehovah entered into a cross-over covenant with Abraham on the boundary of his new possessions in Canaan.[3] It was on a passover night that Lot welcomed the angel visitors to his home in Sodom.[4] It was at the passover season that the Israelites crossed the threshold of their new home in Canaan, when the walls of Jericho fell down, and the blood-colored thread on the house of Rahab was a

---

[1] Exod. 212-6.

[2] Talmud Babyl., *Qiddusheen*, fol. 22,b.

[3] Gen. 15:1-21. See pp. 186-188, supra.

[4] Gen. 19:1-25.

symbol of the covenant of the Hebrew spies with her and her household.[1] The protection of the Israelites against the Middianites,[2] and the Assyrians,[3] and the Medes and the Persians,[4] and again the final overthrow of Babylon, all these events were said to have been at the passover season.[6] These traditions would seem to show that the pass-over covenant was deemed a crossover covenant, and a covenant of welcome at the family and the national threshold.

In the passover rite as observed by modern Jews, at a certain stage of the feast the outer door is opened, and an extra cup and chair are arranged at the table, in the hope that God's messenger will cross the threshold, and enter the home as a welcome guest.[7] All this points to the meaning of "cross-over," and not of "pass-by."

In some parts of northern and eastern Europe there is a custom still preserved among the Jews of jumping over a tub of water on passover night, which is said to be symbolic of crossing the Red Sea, but which shows that the passover

---

[1] Compare Josh. 2:1-20; 5:10-12; 6:12-17.

[2] Judg. 7:1-25.

[3] 2 Kings 19:20-36; 2 Chron. 32:1-22.

[4] Esther 9:12-19.

[5] Dan. 5:1-30.

[6] Edersheim's *Temple: its Ministry and Services*, p.196f.

[7] Edersheim's *the Temple: its Ministry and Services*, p.197; *Home and Synagogue of Modern Jew*, pp.159-161; Ginsbursgh's art. Passover," in Kitto's *Cycl. of Bib.Lit.*

feast was a feast of crossing over.[1]

5. MARRIAGE OF JEHOVAH WITH ISRAEL.

It seems clear that the Egyptian passover rite was a rite of threshold covenanting, as ordered of God and as understood by the Israelites. Its sacrifice was on the threshold of the homes of the Hebrews on the threshold of a new year,[2] and on the threshold of a new nationality. Then Israel began anew in all things. Moreover, it was recognized as the rite of marriage between Jehovah and Israel; as the very Threshold Covenant had its origin in the rite of primitive marriage.

That first passover night was the night when Jehovah took to himself in covenant union the "Virgin of Israel," and became a Husband unto her. From that time forward any recognition of, or affiliation with, another God, is called "whoredom," "adultery," or "fornication."[3] In this light it is that the prophets always speak of idolatry.

Jeremiah recognizes the first passover night as the time of this marriage covenant, when he says:

[1] On the testimony of Rev. Dr. Marcus Jastrow.

[2] Exod. 12:1,2; Lev. 23:5; 9:1,2.

[3] See, for example, Exod. 34:12-16; Lev. 17:7; 20:5-8; Num. 15:39,40; Deut. 31:16; Judg. 2:17; 8: 27, 33; 2 Kings 9:22, 23; I Chron. 5:25; 2 Chron. 21:11; Psa. 73:27; 106:38,39; Isa. 57:3; Jer. 3:1-15, 20; 13:27; Ezek. 6:9; 16:1-63; 20:30; 23:1-49; Hos. 1:2; 2:2; 3:1; 4:12-19; 5:3, 4; 6:6, 7, 10.

"Behold, the days come, saith Jehovah,
That I will make a new covenant
With the house of Israel, and with the house of Judah;
Not according to the covenant that I made with their fathers
In the day that I took them by the hand
To bring them out of the land of Egypt;
Which my covenant they brake,
Although I was an husband unto them, saith Jehovah."[1]

And Jehovah, speaking through Ezekiel of his loving choice of the Hebrew daughter of the Amorite and the Hittite, says: "Now when I passed by thee, and looked upon thee, behold, thy time was the time of love; and I spread my skirt over thee, and covered thy nakedness; yea, I sware unto thee, and entered into a covenant with thee, saith the Lord God, and thou becamest mine."[2]

It seems to be in recognition of the truth that the Egyptian passover was the rite of marriage between Jehovah and Israel, that the Song of Songs, the epithalamium of the Hebrew Scriptures, is always read in the synagogue at the passover service. This idea of the relation of Jehovah and Israel runs through the entire Old Testament, and shows itself in the Jewish ritual of today.

In the primitive marriage rite the stamp of the red hand of the bridegroom is the certification of the covenant union, at the doorway of the family. But in the Egyptian passover it was the virgin of Israel who certified to the marriage covenant by the bloody stamp on the doorway. Hence it

---

[1] Jer. 31:31,32; also Heb. 8:8,9

[2] Ezek. 16:8.

was a feminine symbol, in a bush of hyssop, that was dipped in the blood and used for this stamping.[1] The tree, or bush, is a universal symbol of the feminine in nature. This is shown, for example, in the tree or brush-topped pole as the symbol of Ashtaroth, "wife,"[2] as over against the pillar or obelisk as the symbol of Baal, or "lord," or "husband."[3]

[1] Exod. 12:22.

[2] W. Robertson Smith's *Religion of the Semites*, pp.169-176, and Stade's Geschichte, p.460.

[3] Compare Exod. 34:12-16; Deut. 7:5;12:3; Judg. 3:7; 2 Kings 23:4, 2 Chron. 33:3, etc.

VI.

CHRISTIAN PASSOVER.

1. OLD COVENANT AND NEW.

In the New Testament the rites and symbols of the Old Testament find recognition and explanation. This is peculiarly true of the passover service. It was a central fact in the gospel story. The sacrifice, or offering, of Jesus Christ as the Saviour, was made at that season;[1] and it was evident that he himself felt that it was essential that this be so. He held back from Jerusalem until the approach of the passover feast, when he knew that his death was at hand.[2] And his last passover meal was made the basis of the new memorial and symbolic covenant meal with his disciples.[3] The passover sacrifice is as prominent in the New Testament as in the Old.

Paul, familiar with Jewish customs by study and experience, writing to Corinthian Christians of their duty and privileges as members of the household of faith, urges

---

[1] Matt. 26:1-5; John 13:1.

[2] Matt. 16:21; 26:17,18; John 2:13; 7:1-9.

[3] Matt. 26:17-30; Mark 14:12-28; Luke 22:7-20.

197

them to make a new beginning in their lives, as the Israelites made a new beginning on the threshold of every year at the passover festival, with its accompanying feast of unleavened bread, when all the lay-over leaven from a former state was put away. "Purge out the old leaven," he says, "that ye may be a new lump, even as ye are unleavened. For our passover also hath been sacrificed, even Christ."[1]

2. PROFFERED WELCOME BY THE FATHER.

The primitive passover sacrifice was an offering of blood by the head of the household on the threshold of his home, as a token of his welcome to the guest who would cross over that blood and thereby become one with the family within. It was not an outsider or a stranger who proffered a threshold sacrifice, but it was the house-father who thus extended a welcome to one who was yet outside. The welcoming love was measured by the preciousness of the sacrifice. The richer the offering, the heartier the welcome.[2]

In the Egyptian passover the threshold sacrifice was a proffer of welcome to Jehovah by the collective family in each Hebrew home. In the Christian passover it was the sacrifice of the Son of God on the threshold of the Father's home, the home of the family of the redeemed, as a proffer

---

[1] I Cor. 5:7,8

[2] See pp. 3-5, supra.

of welcome to whoever outside would cross the outpoured blood, and become a member of the family within. Therefore it is written: "God so loved the world, that he gave his only begotten Son, that whosoever believeth on him should not perish, but have eternal life." [1] And "for this cause," says Paul, "I bow my knees unto the Father, from whom every family in heaven and on earth is named."[2]

Among primitive peoples, as among the Jews, no indignity could equal the refusal of a proffered guest-welcome, in a rude trampling on the blood of the threshold sacrifice, instead of crossing over it reverently as a mode of its acceptance. Hence the peculiar force of the words of the Jewish-Christian writer of the Epistle to the Hebrews, concerning the mistreatment of God's threshold sacrifice, in the Son of God offered as our passover: *"A man that hath set at nought Moses' law dieth without compassion on the word of two or three witnesses: of how much sorer punishment, think ye, shall he be judged worthy, who hath **trodden under foot the Son of God,** and hath counted the blood of the covenant, wherewith he was sanctified [separated from the outside world], an unholy [a common] thing, and hath done despite unto the Spirit of grace?"* [3]

---

[1]   John 3:16.

[2]   Eph. 3:14,15.

[3]   Heb. 10:28, 29.

3. BRIDEGROOM AND BRIDE.

All through the New Testament, Jesus, the outpouring of whose blood is "our passover" welcome from the Father, is spoken of as the Bridegroom, and his church as the Bride. His coming to earth is referred to as the coming of the Bridegroom—as was the coming of Jehovah to the Virgin of Israel in Egypt. He likened himself to a bridegroom. And his coming again to his church is foretold as the meeting of the Bridegroom and the Bride.

John the Baptist, forerunner of Jesus, speaking of his mission as closing, and that of Jesus as opening out gloriously, says: "Ye yourselves bear me witness, that I said, I am not the Christ, but, that I am sent before him. He that hath the bride is the bridegroom: but the friend of the bridegroom, which standeth and heareth him, rejoiceth greatly because of the bridegroom's voice; this my joy therefore is fulfilled. He must increase, but I must decrease."[1]

Jesus referring to the charge against his disciples, that they did not fast, as did the disciples of John, said: "Can the sons of the bride-chamber mourn, as long as the bridegroom is with them? but the days will come, when the bridegroom shall be taken away from them, and then will they fast."[2]

Paul repeatedly refers to this relation between Christ

---

[1] John 3:28-30.

[2] Matt. 9:14, 15; Mark 2:19, 20; Luke 5:34, 35.

and his church: "The head of every man is Christ; and the head of the woman is the man; and the head of Christ is God." [1] "The husband is the head of the wife, as Christ also is the head of the church . . . Husbands, love your wives, even as Christ also loved the church, and gave himself up for it . . . He that loveth his own wife loveth himself: for no man ever hated his own flesh; but nourisheth and cherisheth it, even as Christ also the church; because we are members of his body. For this cause shall a man leave his father and mother, and shall cleave to his wife; and the twain shall become one flesh. This mystery is great; but I speak in regard of Christ and of the church." [2]

In the Apocalypse, the inspired seer looking into the future, at the consummation of the present age, tells of the glorious vision before him, when Christ shall come to claim his own: "I heard as it were the voice of a great multitude, and as the voice of many waters, and as the voice of mighty thunders, saying, Hallelujah: for the Lord our God, the almighty, reigneth. Let us rejoice and be exceeding glad, and let us give the glory unto him: for the marriage of the Lamb is come, and his wife hath made herself ready. And it was given unto her that she should array herself in fine linen, bright and pure: for the fine linen is the righteous acts of the saints. And he saith unto me, Write, Blessed are they which are bidden to the marriage supper of the Lamb." [3]

---

[1] I Cor. 11:3.

[2] Eph. 5:23-33.

[3] Rev. 19:6-9.

And again he says: "I saw the holy city, new Jerusalem, coming down out of heaven from God, made ready as a bride adorned for her husband. . . .And there came one of the seven angels . . . and he spake with me, saying, Come hither, I will show thee the bride, the wife of the Lamb. And he carried me away in the Spirit to a mountain great and high, and shewed me the holy city Jerusalem, coming down out of heaven from God, having the glory of God . . . having a wall great and high; having twelve gates. And I saw no temple therein: for the Lord God the Almighty, and the Lamb, are the temple thereof . . . And the gates thereof shall in no wise be shut by day (for there shall be no night there): and they shall bring the glory and as the honor of the nations into it: and there shall in no wise enter into it anything unclean, or he that maketh an abomination and a lie: but only they which are written in the Lamb's book of life."[1]

A closing declaration of the seer is, that the church as the Bride, with the representative of the Bridegroom until his coming, waits and calls for his return: "The spirit and the bride say, Come . . . Come, Lord Jesus."[2] And so, from the Pentateuch to the Apocalypse, the Scriptures, Hebrew and Christian, recognize and emphasize the primitive Threshold Covenant as the beginning of religious rites, and as symbolic of the spirit of all true covenant worship.

[1] Rev. 21:1, 2-9, 12, 22-27.

[2] Ibid., 22:17, 20.

4. SURVIVALS OF THE RITE.

Survivals of the primitive Threshold Covenant are found in various customs among Oriental Christians, and Christians the world over. Thus Easter is still looked at in some regions as the continuance of Passover, and the blood on the threshold is an accompaniment of the feast. Among the modern Greeks, each family, as a rule, buys a lamb, kills it, and eats it on Easter Sunday. "In some country districts the blood [of the lamb] is sometimes smeared on the threshold of the house."[1] Easter, like the Jewish Passover, is the threshold of the new ecclesiastical year.

At the Church of the Holy Sepulcher, in Jerusalem, a principal incident in the Easter festivities is the bringing down of fire from heaven at the opening of the new ecclesiastical year.[2] This ceremony seems to be a survival of the primitive custom of seeking new life, in its symbol of fire, at the threshold of the home and of the new year, in the East and in the West. [3]

In the sacredness of the rite of the primitive Threshold Covenant there is added emphasis to the thought which causes both the Roman Catholic Church and the Greek

---

[1] J. G. Frazer in *Folk-Lore Journal*, I., 275.

[2] See Maundrel's *Journey*, pp.127-131; Hasselquist's *Voyages and Travels*, pp. 136-138; Thomson's *Land and Book*, II., 556f.; Stanley's *Sinai and Palestine*, pp. 464-469.

[3] See pp. 22f., 39-44, supra.

Church to count marriage itself a sacrament. And thus again to the claim that a virgin who is devoted to a religious life is a "spouse of Christ," and that her marriage to an earthly husband is adultery.[1] Many another religious custom points in the same direction.

---

[1] See **Smith and Cheetham's** *Dict. Of Christian Antiq.*, art. "Nun."

VII.

OUTGROWTHS AND PERVERSIONS
OF THIS RITE.

1. ELEMENTAL BEGINNINGS.

Apart from the mooted question of the origin and development of man as man,—whether it be held that he came into being as an incident in the evolutionary progress of the ages, or that his creation was by a special fiat of the Author of all things,—it is obvious that there was a beginning, when man first appeared as a higher order of being than the lower animals then in existence. The distinguishing attribute of man, as distinct from the lower animals at their best, is the capacity to conceive of spiritual facts and forces. Even at his lowest estate man is never without an apprehension of immaterial and supernatural personalities, intangible yet real and potent. The lower animals at their highest, and under the most effective training, give no indication of the possibility of such a conception on their part.

Both the Bible record and the disclosed facts of science show man at the start in a primitive state, with only elemental beginnings of knowledge or thought or skill. No claim is made for him, by any advocate of his pre-eminence in creation, that he then had skill in the arts, or attainment in civilization, or that he was possessed of a religious theory or ritual of even the simplest character. It is a matter of interest and importance to trace the course of man's progress from the first to the present time, and to see how the good and the evil showed themselves along the line, from the same germs of thought and conduct rightly used or misused. The primitive rite of the Threshold Covenant, here brought out as initial and germinative, seems to present a reasonable solution of the observed course in religious development and in religious perversions in the history of mankind from the beginning until now.

Before primitive man could have concerned himself seriously with the course of the heavenly bodies, or the changes of the seasons, or the points of compass and the correspondent shifting of the winds, he must have recognized the sacred mystery of life and its transmission. It would seem that a covenant involved with power from the Author of life for the transmission of life, must have been the primal religious rite that brought man's personal action into the clear light of a covenant relation with his Creator. Every subsequent development of the religious idea, good and bad, pure and impure, would seem to be traceable as an outgrowth, or as a perversion, of this elemental religious rite.

2. MAIN OUTGROWTHS

It would seem clear that the primal idea of a covenant union between two persons, and between those persons and their God, was found in the initial and primitive rite of marriage, with its outpoured blood, or gift of life, on the threshold of being; and that this rite contained in itself the germs of covenanting and of sacrifice, and the idea of an altar and a sacrament, where, and by which, man and God were brought into loving communion and union. Thus the beginning of religious rites was found in the primal Threshold Covenant as here portrayed.

Out of this beginning came all that is best and holiest in the thought of sacrifice and sacrament and spiritual communion. The very highest development of religious truth, under the guidance of progressive revelation from God, and of man's growth in thought and knowledge with the passing ages, is directly in the line of this simple and germinal idea. Both the Bible record and the record of outside history tend to confirm this view of religious rites in their beginning and progress.

New life as a consequence of blood, or life, surrendered in holy covenanting, is a natural inference or outgrowth of the truth of the primal Threshold Covenant. Thus the thought of life after death, in the resurrection or in metempsychosis, comes with the recognition of the simple fact of the results of covenant union in the sight, and with the blessing, of the Author of life, in the rite of the Threshold Covenant.[1]

The transference of the altar of threshold covenanting, from the persons of the primary pair in the family to the hearthstone or entrance threshold of the home or family doorway, with the accompaniment of fire as a means of giving and sustaining life to those who sat at the common

---

[1] See "*Blood Covenant*," pp. 310-313.

table or altar, in the covenant meal or sacrament of hospitality, brought about the custom of sacramental communion feasts with guests human and divine. And so, also, there came the rites of worship, with the altar of burnt sacrifice or of incense, and the marriage torch, and the doorway fire, and the threshold or hearthstone covenant at a wedding. Out of this thought there came gradually and naturally the prominence of the altar and the altar fire in private and public worship, as it obtains both in the simpler and in the more gorgeous ecclesiastical rituals.[1]

In conjunction with the place of fire on the family altar in the Threshold Covenant, there came naturally the recognition of fire and warmth and light as gifts of God for the promotion and preservation of life to those who were dependent on him. Thus the sun as the life-giving fire of the universe came to be recognized as a manifestation of God's power and love. Its agency in bringing new life after death, in the course of the changing seasons, led men to connect the movements of the heavenly bodies with God's dealings with man in the line of his covenant love. The too common mistake has been of thinking of this view of celestial nature as the origin of man's religious rites, instead of as an outgrowth of the primal religious rite, which antedated man's study of, or wonder over, the workings of the elements and the course of the heavenly bodies.

In summing up the results of such a study as this, of primitive customs and their outgrowth, it is necessary only to suggest a few of the more prominent lines of progress

---

[1] See pp. 22f., 39-44, 99-164, supra.

from the elemental beginning, leaving it to the student and thinker to follow out these, and to find others, in his more careful and further consideration of the subject in its varied ramifications. It is sufficient now to affirm that the Old Testament and the New point to this primitive rite of the Threshold Covenant as a basis of their common religious ritual, and that gleams of the same germinal idea show themselves in the best features of all the sacred books of the ages. It would be easy, did time and space allow, to follow out in detail the indications that all modes of worship in sacrifice, in oblation, in praise, and prayer, in act and in word, are but natural expressions of desire for covenant union with Deity, and of joy in the thought of its possession, as based on the fact of such covenanting sought and found in the primal religious rite of the human race.

3. CHIEF PERVERSIONS.

With the world as it is, and with man as he is, every possibility of good has a corresponding possibility of evil. Good perverted becomes evil. Truth which, rightly used, proves a savor of life, will, when misused, prove a savor of death.[1] And that which is a symbol of truth becomes a means of misleading when looked at as if it were in itself the truth.

The primitive Threshold Covenant as an elemental religious rite was holy and pure, and had possibilities of outgrowth in the direction of high spiritual attainment and

---

[1] 2 Cor. 2:16.

aspiring. But the temptation to uplift the agencies in this rite into objects deemed of themselves worthy of worship resulted in impurity and deterioration, by causing the symbol to hide the truth instead of disclosing it.

Among the earliest forms of a temple as a place of worship was the ziggurat, or stepped pyramid, erected as a mighty altar, with its shrine, or holy of holies, at the summit, wherein a bride of the gods awaited the coming of the deity to solemnize the primal Threshold Covenant in expression of his readiness to enter into loving communion with the children of men.[1] From this custom the practice of Threshold Covenanting at the temple doorways became incumbent on women of all conditions of society at certain times, and under certain circumstances, in certain portions of the world, as a proof of their religious devotion,[2] and thus there grew up all the excesses of sacred prostitution in different portions of the world.[3]

The prominence given to the two factors in the primitive Threshold Covenant as a sacred religious act, led to the perversion of the original idea by making the factors themselves objects of reverence and worship and separately, or together, they came to be worshiped with impure and degrading accompaniments.

---

[1] See, for example, Heridotins' *History*, Bk. I., chaps. 181, 182. See pp. IIIf., supra.

[2] Herodotus' *History*, Bk. I., chap. 199.

[3] See Deut. 25:1-9. See, also, chapter on "Sacred Prostitution" in Wake's *Serpent Worship*; and Prof. W. M. Ramsay's "Holy City of Phrygia," in *Contemporary Review* for October, 1893.

Reverence for the phallus, or for phallic emblems, shows itself in the earliest historic remains of Babylonia, Assyria, India, China, Japan, Persia, Phrygia, Phoenicia, Egypt, Abyssinia, Greece, Rome, Germany, Scandinavia, France, Spain, Great Britain, North and South America, and the Islands of the Sea. It were needless to attempt detailed proof of this statement, in view of all that has been written on the subject by historians, archaeologists, and students of comparative religions.[1] It is enough to suggest that the mistake has too often been made of supposing that this "phallic worship" was a primitive conception of a religious truth, instead of a perversion of the earlier and purer idea which is at the basis of the highest religious conceptions, from the beginning until now.

Quite as widely extended, in both time and space, as the worship of the phallus as the symbol of masculine potency, is the recognition of the tree of life as the symbol of feminine nature in its fruit-bearing capacity. A single tree, or a grove of trees, or the lotus flower, the fig, or the pomegranate, with the peculiar form of their seed capsules, appear in all the earlier religious symbolisms, over against the phallus in its realistic or its conventional forms, as

---

[1] See, for example, Squier's *Serpent Symbol*; Forling's *Rivers of Life*; Westropp's and Wake's *Ancient Symbol Worship*; Knight's *Worship of Priapus*; Jennings' *Phallicism;* Frazer's *Golden Bough*; Monier-Williams' *Brahmanism and Hinduism*, and his *Buddism*; Griffis' *Religions of Japan*, etc.

representative of reproductive life. [1]

In ancient Assyrian sculpture the most familiar representation of spiritual blessing was of a winged deity with a basket and a palm cone, touching with the cone a sacred tree, or again the person of a sovereign, as if imparting thereby some special benefit or power. This representation was long a mystery to the archeologist, but a recent scholar has shown that it is an illustration of a practice common in the East today, of carrying a cone of the male palm to a female palm tree, in order to vitalize it by the pollen. [2] The cone is one of the conventional forms of the phallus, worshiped as a symbol in the temples of the goddesses of the East in earlier days and later. [3] Hence this ancient Assyrian representation is an illustration of the truth that the primitive threshold covenant was recognized as the type of divine power, and covenant blessing, imparted to God's representative, under the figure of the phallus and the

---

[1] See, for example, in addition to the books just cited, Fergusson's *Tree and Serpent Worship;* Ohnefalach-Richter's *Kypros, die Bibel und Homer;* Hopkins' *Religions of India*, pp. 527f., 533, 540, 542.

[2] See Dr. E. B. Tyler's article on "The Winged Figures of the Assyrian and other Ancient Monuments," in *Proceedings of the Sac. Of Bib. Arch.* XII., part 8, pp. 383-393; Dr. Bonayia's articles on "Sacred Trees," in "*Babylonian and Oriental Record,* III., Nos. 1-4; IV., Nos. 4, 5; and DeLacouperie's articles on Trees, ibid. IV., Nos. 5, 10, 11.

[3] See, for example, Ohnefalach-Richter's *Kypros*, Tafel-Band, pl. lxxxii., figures 7, 8; Donaldson's *Architectural Medals of Classic Antiquity*, pp. 105-109; VonLoher and Joyner's *Cyprus: Historical and Descriptive*, p. 153f; Perrot and Chipiez's *History of Art in Phoenicia and Cyprus*, I., 123, 276f., 281, 184, 331f.; W. Robertson Smith's *Religion of the Semites*, p. 191.

tree.

It would seem, indeed, that the pillar and the tree came to be the conventional symbols of the male and female elements erected in front of an altar of worship,[1] and that, in the deterioration of the ages, these symbols themselves were worshiped, and their symbolism was an incentive to varied forms of impurity, instead of to holy covenanting with God and in God's service. Therefore these symbols were deemed by true worshipers a perversion of an originally sacred rite, and their destruction was a duty with those who would restore God's worship to its pristine purity.

Thus the command to Jehovah's people as to their treatment of the people of Canaan was: "Take heed to thyself, lest thou make a covenant with the inhabitants of the land whither thou goest, lest it be for a snare in the midst of thee; but ye shall break down their altars, and dash to pieces their pillars [or male symbols], and ye shall cut down their Asherim [or trees as a female symbol]: for thou shalt worship no other god: for the Lord [Jehovah], whose name is Jealous, is a jealous God: lest thou make a covenant with the inhabitants of the land, and they go a whoring after their gods."[2] Here is a distinct reference to the primitive Threshold Covenant in its purity and sacredness, and to its perversion in the misuse of the phallus and tree in their symbolism.

Again the command was explicit to the Israelites: "Thou shalt not plant thee an Asherah of any kind of tree

---

[1] Compare W. Robertson Smith's *Religion of the Semites,* p. 437f.

[2] Exod. 34:12-15; Deut. 7:5.

beside the altar of the Lord thy God, which thou shalt make thee. Neither shalt thou set thee up a pillar; which the Lord thy God hateth." [1]

From the earliest historic times the serpent seems to have been accepted as a symbol of the nexus of union between the two sexes, and to be associated, therefore, with the pillar and the tree, as suggestive of the desire that may be good or evil, according to its right or wrong direction and use. Its place as a symbol has been at the threshold of palace and temple and home, with limitless powers of evil in its misuse. [2]

"Mighty snakes standing upright," together with "mighty bulls of bronze" were "on the threshold of the gates" in ancient Babylon. [3] A serpent wreathed the phallus boundary stone (as if suggestive of its being a thing of life)

---

[1] Deut. 16:21,22.

[2] There seems, indeed, to be a connection between the Hebrew words, *Miphtan*, "threshold," and *pethen*, "asp," "adder," or "serpent," as first pointed out to me by Mr. Montague Cockle. Although the verbal root is not preserved in the Hebrew, there is no valid reason for doubting that they go back to the same root. In Arabic, the verb is preserved as *pathana*, "to tempt," Its derivations indicate the same meaning. This would seem to confirm the connection of the primitive threshold, the serpent, and temptation. In Leland's *Etruscan Roman Remains* (p. 131f.) are citations from several ancient works, and references to current Italian traditions, showing the supposed connection of the serpent with the threshold, the phallus, and married life, that are in obvious confirmation of the views here expressed.

[3] See p. 109f., supra; also, Schrader's *Keilinschriftliche Bibliothek*, Vol. III., Pt.2, p. 72f.

on the threshold of Babylonian domains.[1]

In the representation of Nergal, the lord of the under world, in the ancient Babylonian mythology, the phallus and the serpent were identical.[2] Beltis-Allat, consort of Nergal, and lady of the under world, brandished a serpent in either hand. She was guardian of the waters of life which were under the threshold of the entrance of her realm.[3]

That which was primarily a holy instinct became, in its perversion, a source of evil and a cause of dread, hence the serpent became a representative of evil itself, and the conflict with it was the conflict between good and evil, between light and darkness. This is shown in the religions of ancient Babylonia, Egypt, and India, and Phoenicia and Greece, and Mexico and Peru, and various other countries.[4]

Vishnoo and his wife Lakshmi, from whom, according to Hindoo teachings, the world was produced, and by whom it continues or must cease, are represented as seated on a

[1] See Wilkinson's *Anc. Egypt.*, III., 235, pl. lv., fig.2. Prisse's *Mon. Egypt*, pl. xxxvii.; also Layard's *Nineveh and its Remains*, p.169 (Am.ed.), and W. Max Müller's *Asien and Europa*, p. 314.

[2] See Perrot and Chipiez's *History of Art in Chaldea and Assyria*, I., 349f. See, also Layard's *Monuments*, Series II., pl. 5, for representation of the conflict between Marduk and Tiamat. The serpent is there shown on the feminine Tiamai where it appears on the masculine Nergal.

[3] See Maspero's *Dawn of Civilization*, pp. 690-696; Sayce's *Relig. Of Anc. Babylonia*, p. 286.

[4] See Sayce's *Relig. Of Anc. Babylonia*, pp.281-283; Wilkinson's *Anc. Egypt.*, III., 141-155; Fergusson's *Tree and Serpent Worship*, pp. 5-72; Squier's *Serpent Symbol*, pp. 137-254; Reville's *Native Religions of Mexico and Peru*, pp. 29-32, 53, 166.

serpent, as the basis of their life and power.[1] Siva, also, giver and destroyer of life, is crowned with a serpent, and a serpent is his necklace, while the symbol of his worship is the *linga in yoni*.[2] A mode of Hindoo worship includes the placing of a stone *linga* between two serpents, and under two trees, the one a male tree and the other a female tree.[3] And in various ways the serpent appears, in connection with different Hindoo deities, as the agent of life giving or of life-destroying.[4] A suggestive representation of Booddha as the conqueror of desire shows him seated restfully on a coiled serpent, the hooded head of which is a screen or canopy above his head.[5]

Apollo, son of Zeus, was the slayer of the man-destroying serpent at Delphi; yet the serpent, when conquered, became a means of life and inspiration to others.[6] Aesculapius, the god of healing, a son of Apollo, was represented by the serpent because he gave new life to those who were dying. Serpents were everywhere connect-

---

[1] See Wilkins' *Hindu Mythology*, p.99.

[2] See Wilkins' *Hindu Mythology*, p.218.

[3] Maurice's *Indian Antiq.*, V.182f.

[4] Ibid., V.

[5] See frontispiece of Sir Monier Monier-Williams' *Buddhism*; see also, Fergusson's article on "The Amravati Tope" in "Journal of the Royal Asiatic Society," Vol. III., Pt.I, pp. 132-166.

[6] See Keightley's *Mythology*, art."Phoebus-Apollo."

ed with his worship as a means of healing.[1] The female oracle who represented Apollo at Delphi sat on a tripod formed of entwined serpents.[2] Serpents on the head of Medusa were a means of death to the beholder; and these serpents were given to Medusa instead of hair because of her faithlessness and sacrilege in the matter of the Threshold Covenant.[3] Thus the good and the evil in that which the serpent symbolized were shown in the religions of the nations of antiquity, and serpent worship became one of the grossest perversions of the idea of the primitive Threshold Covenant.

As in the matter of phallic worship and tree worship, so in this of the worship of the serpent, it would seem unnecessary to multiply illustrations of its prominence in various lands, when so many special treatises on the subject are already available.[4] It is only necessary to emphasize anew the fact that the evident thought of the symbol is an outgrowth or a perversion of the idea of the primitive Threshold Covenant.

The form of the Bible narrative, portraying the first temptation and the first sin, seems to show how early the symbolism of the tree and the serpent was accepted in popular speech. From that narrative as it stands it would

---

[1] See "Aesculapius," in Smith's *Classical Dictionary*.

[2] See Herodotus' *History*, Bk. IX., chap.81.

[3] See "Gorgones," in Smith's *Classical Dictionary*.

[4] See, for example, Maurice's *Indian Antiquities*; Fergusson's *Tree and Serpent Worship;* Forlong's *Rivers of Life*, I.,93-322; Wake's *Serpent Worship*, pp.81-106.

appear that the first act of human disobedience was incontinence, in transgression of a specific command to abstain, at least for a time, from carnal intercourse. Desire, as indicated by the serpent, prompted to an untimely partaking of the fruit of the forbidden tree, and the consequences of sin followed. The results of this act of disobedience, as recorded in the sacred text, [1] make evident the correctness of this view of the case. When the Bible narrative was first written, whenever that was, the terms "tree,"[2] "fruit of the tree,"[3] "knowledge,"[4] "serpent," were familiar figures of speech or euphemisms, and their use in the Bible narrative would not have been misunderstood by readers generally. Probably there was no question as to this for many centuries. It was not until the dull prosaic literalism of the Western mind obscured the meaning of Oriental figures of speech that there was any general doubt as to what was affirmed in the Bible story of the first temptation and disobedience.[5]

Philo Judaeus at the beginning of the Christian era, seems to understand this as the meaning of the narrative in Genesis, and he applies the teachings of that narrative

---

[1] Gen. 3:7,10-13,16.

[2] See, for example, Psa. 128:3; Prov. 3:18; 11:30; Ezek. 19:16.

[3] See, for example, Gen. 30:2; Deut. 7:13; 28:4, 18, 53; 30:9; Psa. 127:3; 132:11; Song of Songs 4:16; Isa. 13:18; Micah 5:7; Acts 2:39.

[4] See, for example, Gen. 4:1, 17, 15; 38:26; Judg. 11:39; 19:25; I Sam. 1:19; I Kings 1:4; Matt. 1:25.

[5] Gen. 3:1-13.

accordingly.[1] There are indications that the rabbis looked similarly at the meaning of the Bible text. There are traces of this traditional view in different Jewish writings.[2]

Evidently the original meaning was still familiar in the early Christian ages. But its becoming connected with false doctrines and heresies, as taught by the Ophites and other Gnostic sects, seems to have brought the truth itself into disrepute, and finally led to its repudiation in favor of a dead literalism.[3] The curse resting on the serpent, in consequence of the first sin of incontinence, was the degradation of the primitive impulse,[4] unless uplifted again by divine inspiration.[5] Because of their breach of the covenant of divine love our first parents were expelled from their home of happiness, and the guardians of the threshold forbade their return to it.[6]

In the closing chapters of the New Testament, as in the opening chapters of the Old, the symbolism of the tree and the serpent, and the covenant relations involved in crossing

---

[1] See, for example, Philo Judaeus' *Works*, "On the Creation," I.,53-60; "On the Allegories of the Sacred Laws," I., 15-20; "Questions and Solutions," I., 31-41.

[2] See, for example, *Midrasch Bereschit Rabba*, pararshah 18.§6, in comments on Gen. 2:25; Weber's *Die Lehren d. Talmud* (ed. 1866), pp. 210-213.

[3] See Clement of Alexandria's *Miscellanies*, III.,17; also Irenaeus's *Against Heresies*, I.,30.

[4] Gen. 3:14,15.

[5] Compare Num. 21:4-9; 2 Kings 18:4; John 3:14, 15.

[6] Gen. 3:22-24.

the threshold, appear as familiar and well-understood figures of speech. "The dragon, the old serpent, which is the Devil and Satan,"[1] representing unholy desire, is shut out from the precincts of the New Jerusalem. Within the gates of that city is there the tree of life watered by the stream that flows from under the throne of power.[2] The city threshold is the dividing line between light and darkness, good and evil, life and death. "Blessed are they that wash their robes, that they may have the right to come to the tree of life, and may enter in by the gates into the city. Without are the dogs, and the sorcerers, and the fornicators, and the murderers, and the idolators, and everyone that loveth and maketh a lie."[3]

Thus it is in the Hebrew and Christian Scriptures, at their beginning and at their close. And there are traces of the same truth in the teachings of the various religions, and of the more primitive customs and symbolisms. The all-dividing threshold separates the within from the without; and a covenant welcome there gives one a right to enter in through the gates into the eternal home, to be a partaker of the tree of life, with its ever-renewing and revivifying fruits.

---

[1] Rev. 20:1, 2.

[2] *Ibid.*, 21:1-27; 22:1, 2.

[3] *Ibid.*, 22:14,15.

APPENDIX

[Publisher's Note: the Latin Appendix has not been included in this edition, since it would not benefit most modern readers.]

BIBLE TESTIMONY.

A distinct reference to the proofs of chastity, in the blood-stamped cloth, is found in the Bible record of the ancient law of Israel. *"If any man take a wife, and go in unto her, and hate her, and lay shameful things to her charge, and bring up an evil name upon her, and say, I took this woman, and when I came nigh to her, I found not in her the tokens of virginity: then shall the father of the damsel, and her mother, take and bring forth the tokens of the damsel's virginity unto the elders of the city in the gate: and the damsel's father shall say unto the elders, I gave my daughter unto this man to wife, and he hateth her; and, lo, he hath laid shameful things to her charge, saying, I found not in thy daughter the tokens of virginity; and yet these are the tokens of my daughter's virginity. And they shall spread the garment* (or cloth, Hebrew *simlah*) *before the elders of the city."*

"And the elders of that city shall take the man and chastise him; and they shall amerce him in an hundred shekels of silver, and give them unto the father of the damsel, because he hath brought up an evil name upon a

virgin of Israel: and she shall be his wife; he may not put her away all his days. But if this thing be true, that the tokens of virginity were not found in the damsel: then they shall bring out the damsel to the doors of her father's house, and the men of the city shall stone her with stones that she die: because she hath wrought folly in Israel, to play the harlot in her father's house."[1]

WOMAN AS A DOOR.

In different languages and among various peoples there is, as already suggested,[2] an apparent connection between the terms, and the corresponding ideas, of "woman" and "door," that would seem to be a confirmation of the fact that the earliest altar was at the threshold of the woman, and of the door.

Thus, in the Song of Songs 8:8,9:—

> *"We have a little sister,*
> *And she hath no breasts:*
> *What shall we do for our sister*
> *In the day when she shall be spoken for?*
> *If she be a wall,*
> *We will build upon her a turret of silver:*
> *And if she be a door,*
> *We will inclose her with boards of cedar."*

Job, cursing the day of his birth, says (Job 3:1-10)

---

[1] Deut. 22:13-21.

[2] See, for example, 197f., supra.

"Let the day perish wherein I was born,
And the night which said, There is a man child conceived
Neither let it behold the eyelids of the morning:
Because it shut not up the doors of my mother's womb,
Nor hid trouble from mine eyes."

Referring to this passage, the Babylonian Talmud (Treatise Bechoroth, 45 *a*) quotes Rabbi Eliezer as saying, "Just as a house has doors, so also a woman has doors." Others say: "Just as a house has keys (*miphteakh*, literally 'opener'), so the woman has a key; for it is said (Gen. 30:22) 'God hearkened to her, and opened [a play upon *patakh*, 'to open,' and *miphteakh*, 'key'] her womb.'" The famous Rabbi Akibah says: "just as a house has hinges, so there are hinges to a wife; for it is written (I Sam. 4:19), 'She kneeled and gave birth, for her hinges had turned' [(translating *sîrîm* (or *tseereem*) as 'hinges' instead of 'pains'; the word has the former meaning in Proverbs 26:14. 'As the door turneth upon its hinges, so doth the sluggard upon his bed.')]"

The Talmudic treatise Middâ (Mishna § 2, 5) explains the different parts of the womb under the metaphors *khêder*, "interior chamber;" *p'rosdôr*, "vestibule;" *'aliyyâ*, "upper story."[1] Professor Dr. Morris Jastrow, Jr., in citing these metaphors, suggests that they coincide with the Arabic and Egyptian custom of using a key in the marriage rite.

Critics have long puzzled over the seemingly contradictory uses of the Hebrew word *pôth* in two places in the Old Testament; and the connection of "woman" and

---

[1] See also citations from Buxtorf at p. 200, supra.

"door" with the parts thereof, above suggested, may aid in resolving the difficulty. At I Kings 7:50, in a list of the holy vessels of the house of the Lord, there are mentioned "the hinges (Heb., *pôthôth*), both for the doors of the inner house, the most holy place, and for the doors of the house, to wit, of the temple, of gold." At Isaiah 3:17 the same word *pôth* is translated "their secret parts," in a reference to the humiliation of "the daughters of Zion." It has been suggested by some that there was a corruption of the text in Isaiah. (See Delitzsch and Dillmann, in their commentaries at this place.) Yet in view of the rabbinical uses of language, the text would seem to be trustworthy, *pôth* is an "opening," of a woman or of a door. Additional light is thrown on the use of the term *pôth* as "opening" and as "hinge," or "socket," when we bear in mind that the hinge of an Oriental door was a hole, or cavity, or door socket, on which the door turned, in order to give an opening or entrance. Often these door sockets were made of metal,—bronze, silver, or gold.[1] Sometimes the entire thresholds, in which were these sockets or "basons," were of metal. If, however, the threshold was of stone or wood, the socket, or a plate with a depression in it, was of metal. The *pôth*, therefore, when referring to a door, was the metal plate or socket in the threshold on which the door turned as on a hinge.

It is, indeed, possible that the opening or cavity in the ancient stone or metal threshold was sometimes the bason,

---

[1] See pp. 127, 132f., 207f., supra.

or vessel, into which the covenanting blood was poured.[1] In that case, the correspondence of the opening of the woman, and the socket of the threshold, would be more obvious. Important inscriptions are usually found at or around these so-called "door sockets," in Babylonian relics and there is still doubt in many minds whether these cavities were always hinge sockets.

The word "hinges," or hangers," is at the best an inaccurate and misleading term, as applied to the pivots or knuckles on which an ancient door swung in its socket. Ancient doors were not hung on hinges, but they swung on pivots. Instead of a hinge, there was a knuckle or pintle, with a corresponding socket, or cavity, or opening, in the threshold or door-sill. Both Gesenius[2] and Stade give "socket" as one of the meanings of *pôth*. The plural, *pôthôth*, of course, refers to the sockets of two leaves of a double door on one threshold.

When Samson was shut in at Gaza by the Philistines, the double leaves of the city gate were held together by a bar, without the lifting of which the doors could not be opened. "And Samson lay till midnight, and arose at midnight, and laid hold of the doors of the gate of the city, and the two posts (the upright stiles, at the bottom of which were the knuckles that turned in the threshold sockets) , and plucked them up, bar (cross-bar or latch) and all, and put them upon his shoulders, and carried them up to the top of

[1] See p. 207f., supra.

[2] *Handworterbuch*, Midhan and Volck, 11th ed., s.v.

[3] *Woerterbuch U. Alt. Test.*, s.v.

the mountain that is before Hebron."[1]

I have in my possession a bronze door-socket and knuckle of an ancient gate or door, unearthed from a mound in the vicinity of Ghuzzeh, the site of ancient Gaza, that meets this description.

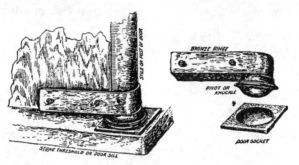

In primitive symbolism, as shown in Babylonia, Egypt, and India, the circle or ring, like this socket, represents woman.

It would be interesting, in this connection, to follow out the meanings and uses of the Greek words (*puthmen*), root (*phu*) and (*phlie*), doorpost, root (*phli*) compare (*phleo*), (*philos*). It is evident that the twofold idea of the threshold of life, and the threshold, or sockets, of the door, is in the uses of these terms and their derivatives in earlier and later Greek. But only this suggestion can be made here.

The correspondence of "woman" and "door," or of "wife" and "threshold," in the Arabic, has already been

---

[1]   Judges 16:3.

pointed out.[1] A similar suggestion is in Sanskrit terms. [2]

In Germany, even at the present time, a common term for "woman" is "woman chamber" (*Frauenzimmer*), as in Arabic *hareema* is a woman, while *hareem* is the women's apartment. A remark attributed to a prominent American clergyman, as showing the naturalness of the figure of woman as a door, is: "He who marries a wife opens a door, through which unborn generations shall troop."

A Chinese character is the representation of "threshold," of "door," and also of "woman."[3] It is suggested by the lexicographer that the origin of this character was a small door in a large gate, as the inner door to the hareem or women's apartments; but it seems probable, from the correspondence of this twofold idea with the primitive thought of woman as the door of humanity, that the Chinese character must have had an origin prior to that degree of civilization which recognized such a classification in household apartments. The combin-ation of "door" and "border" is another Chinese character[4] that stands for "threshold" or "door-sill,"[5] Confucius said that this threshold "should not be trodden on when walking through" the door.

---

[1] See p. 200, supra.

[2] See p. 197f, supra.

[3] *'kw' un*　　　閫

[4] *yü*　　　閾

[5] See S. Wells Williams' *Syllable Dictionary of the Chinese Language*, pp. 496, 1141.

SYMBOLISM OF THE TWO SEXES.

As showing the antiquity, as well as the universality, of the symbolism of the two sexes as the source of life, in connection with reverent worship, an illustration of the ancient Egyptian Book of the Dead is noteworthy. In a vignette on Chapter CXXV, in the Papyrus Ani, a worshiper, is represented before the throne of Osiris, in the Hall of Righteousness, with uplifted hands, in token of covenant worship, while his offering is a lotus flower, the symbol of virility.[1] This vignette is reproduced on the cover of this volume. The lotus flower has the same signification in Assyria and India as in Egypt. [2]

The pine cone, which, as the symbol of virility and vitalizing force, was prominent in the ancient Assyrian sculptures, as also in the Phenician and Grecian cults,[3] was likewise to be found in ancient Rome. An enormous bronze pine cone, eleven feet high, probably older than the Christian era, still ornaments a fountain in the gardens of the Vatican. Lanciani says: "Pope Symmachus, who did so much toward the embellishment of sacred edifices in Rome (between 498 and 514), removed the pine cone from its an-

---

[1] Le Page Renouf's Book of the Dead in *Proceedings of the Society of Biblical Archaeology,* for November, 1895. Plate xxxi.

[2] See pp. 199, 234, supra.

[3] See Barker's *Lares and Penales*; or, *Cilicia and its Governors*, p. 217f.; also see p. 231f., supra.

cient place, most probably from Agrippa's artificial lake in the Campus Martius, and used it for adorning the magnificent fountain which he had built in the center of the so-called 'paradise' of S. Peter's, viz., in the center of the square portico in front of the basilica."[1]

Among the Pompeian relics in the Royal Museum at Naples is a representation of a woman making an offering to Priapus in order to be cured of sterility. She brings a pine cone, while her husband is near her.[2]

Evidence of the fact that boundary posts, landmarks, and milestones were intended to represent the phallus at the threshold in the Roman empire, as in the far East, abound among the same relics in the Neapolitan Museum.[3]

SYMBOLISM OF TREE AND SERPENT.

A striking confirmation of the view taken in this work of the symbolism of the serpent, as the nexus between the two sexes, the female being represented by the fig-tree, and the male by the upright stone, or pole,[4] is found in an ancient religious custom in Mysore, India. Captain J. S. F. Mackenzie contributed an interesting paper on this subject

---

[1] Lanciani's *Ancient Rome,* p. 286f.

[2] Aine's *Herculaneum et Pompei,* Tome VIII, Planche 56, facing p. 221.

[3] *Ibid.,* pl. 24, 25, 27, 30, 39, 41, 44, 48, 54, 55, 56, 59.

[4] See pp. 230-240, supra.

to the "Indian Antiquary,"[1] "Round about Bangalore, more especially towards the Lal Bagh and Petta,—as the native town is called,—three or more stones are to be found together, having representations of serpents carved upon them. These stones are erected always under the sacred fig-tree by some pious person, whose means and piety determine the care and finish with which they are executed. Judging from the number of the stones, the worship of the serpent appears to be more prevalent in the Bangalore district than in other parts of the province. No priest is ever in charge of them. There is no objection to men doing so, but from custom, or for some reason,—perhaps because the serpent is supposed to confer fertility on barren women,—the worshiping of the stones, which takes place during the Gauri feast, is confined to women of all Hindu classes and creeds. The stones, when properly erected, ought to be on a built-up stone platform facing the rising sun, and under the shade of two *peepul* (*Ficus religiosa*) trees,—a male and female growing together, and wedded by ceremonies, in every respect the same as in the case of human beings,—close by, and growing in the same platform a n*imb* (*margosa*) and *bipatra* (a kind of wood-apple), which are supposed to be living witnesses of the marriage. The expense of performing the marriage ceremony is too heavy for ordinary persons, and so we generally find only one *peepul* and a *nimb* on the platform. By the common people these two are supposed to represent man and a wife."

---

[1] Cited in *Notes and Queries*, fifth series, Vol. IV, p. 463.

COVENANT OF THRESHOLD-CROSSING.

An American gentlemen traveling among the Scandinavian immigrants in Wisconsin and Minnesota, was surprised to see their house doors quite generally standing open, as if they had no need of locks and bolts. He argued from this that they were an exceptionally honest people, and that they had no fear of thieves and robbers. A Scandinavian clergyman, being asked about this, said that they had thieves in that region, but that thieves would not cross a threshold, or enter a door, with evil intent, being held back by a super-stitious fear of the consequences of such a violation of the covenant obligation incurred in passing over the threshold.

I asked a native Syrian woman, "if a thief wanted to get into your home to steal from you, would he come in at the door, if he saw that open?" "Oh, no!" she answered, "he would come in at the window, or would dig in from behind." "Why wouldn't he come in at the door?" I asked. "Because his *reverence* would keep him from that," she said, in evident reference to the superstitious dread of crossing a threshold with evil intent,—a dread growing out of an inborn survival of reverence for the primitive altar, with the sacredness of a covenant entered into by its crossing.

The very term commonly employed in the New Testament for thieving indicates the "digging through" a building, instead of entering by the door. "Lay not up for yourselves treasures upon the earth, where moth and rust doth consume, and where thieves break through [literally, dig through; Greek, *diorusso*] and steal."[1] "If the master of the house had known in what hour the thief was coming, he would have watched, and not have left his house to be digged through."[2]

Canon Tristram tells of an Adawan shaykh who was proud of being a "robber," a "highwayman," but who resented the idea that he was a "thief,"—a "sneak thief." "I am not a thief," he said; "I do not dig into the houses of fellaheen in the night. I would scorn it. I only take by force in the day time. And, if God gives me strength, shall I not use it?" Canon Tristram adds: "A 'thief,' as distinguished from a 'robber,' would never think of attempting to force the door, but would noiselessly dig through a wall in the rear,—a work of no great labor, as the walls are generally of earth, or sun dried bricks, or, at best, of stone imbedded in turf instead of in mortar."[3]

A former missionary in Palestine[4] says: "Digging through the wall is the common method pursued by house-breakers in Palestine, and, save in the cities, the operation is not one of great difficulty. Windows, in our sense, do not exist in the houses of the villagers . . . but the walls, built of roughly broken stones and mud, are easily, and by a skilled hand almost noiselessly, penetrated. One night, about

---

[1] Matt. 6:19; also Matt. 6:20.

[2] Luke 12:39; also Matt. 24:43; Exod. 22:2; Ezek. 12:2-7.

[3] See The Sunday School Times for March 7, 1896.

[4] The Rev. William Ewing, in The Sunday School Times for March 7, 1896.

midnight, I was driven from my resting-place under a stunted olive-tree in the plain of Sharon by a terrific thunderstorm, and took refuge in the miserable fellahy village of Kalansaweh. A good woman unbarred her door and admitted me to a single apartment, in which, on the ground level, were several sheep and cattle, with an ass, and on the higher level a pretty large family asleep, all dimly discerned by the light of a little oil lamp stuck in a crevice in the wall. The atmosphere was awful. I asked why they did not have a window or opening in the wall. The woman held up her hands in amazement. 'What!' she exclaimed, 'and assist the robbers [thieves] . . . The robbers ['thieves'], she explained, were the Arabs in the plain. Greater rascals do not exist. They were great experts, she explained, in 'digging through' the houses; to put a window in the wall would only tempt them, and facilitate their work."

Now, as of old, among the more primitive pastoral people of Palestine, "He that entereth not by the door into the fold of the sheep, but climbeth up some other way, the same is a thief and a robber . . . The thief cometh not but that he may steal, and kill, and destroy."[1]

I remember now, what I did not realize the meaning of at the time, that while I was journeying in Arabia we did not set a watch before the entrance of our tents, when we were near a village; but the guards were at the rear of the tents, to watch against thieves, who would crawl underneath the canvas to steal what they might.

It seems to have been a custom in medieval times, and probably earlier, for the besiegers in war time to endeavor

---

[1]   John 10:1, 10.

to enter a city which they would sack through a breach in the walls, or by scaling the walls, rather than by entering the gates. To deliver up the keys of the city gates to a hostile commander was equivalent to capitulating or making formal terms of surrender. In the military museum at Berlin are preserved the keys of cities captured by the emperors of Germany at various times along the centuries.

There is a trace of this custom of besiegers, even in Old Testament times, in the injunctions to Israel with reference to its warfares: "When thou drawest nigh unto a city to fight against it, then proclaim peace unto it [proffer quarter]. And it shall be, if it make thee answer of peace, and open [the gates] unto thee, then it shall be, that all the people that is found therein shall become tributary unto thee, and shall serve thee. And if it will make no peace with thee, but will make war against thee, then thou shalt besiege it: and when the Lord thy God delivereth it into thine hand, thou shalt smite every male thereof with the edge of the sword."[1]

It has been suggested on a former page,[2] but perhaps not sufficiently explained, that this idea of subjecting one's self to the covenant obligations of citizenship by passing through the city gates, over the threshold, had to do with the Grecian custom of welcoming back to his own city the victor in the Olympian games through a breach in the walls, instead of through the gate. The meaning of this Greek custom (continued in Rome) was not clear in the days of Plutarch, and he, in seeking to account for it, suggests that

---

[1] Deut. 20:10-13.

[2] See pp.5-7, supra.

it may have been intended to show that a city having such men among its citizens needed no walls of defense.[1] But, as they rebuilt their walls after the entrance of the victor, this explanation is not satisfactory. The world-wide recognition of the covenant obligations of a passage through a gate over the threshold is a more satisfactory explanation. If the victor, on returning in triumph from the games, were to enter his city through the gates, like any other citizen, he would be subject to the laws of the city as a citizen or a guest; but if the city would recognize him as a conqueror, at home as well as at Olympia, they would let him come in through a breach in the walls. In this act the citizens nominally submitted themselves to him; and a city thus entered, and, as it were, captured, often felt that it received more honor from its victor than it could confer upon him.[2]

DOORKEEPER, AND CARRIER.

A "porter" and a "porter" are two very different persons, as the terms are employed in both Europe and America. We speak of a porter as a menial who carries burdens, such as parcels or baggage, a mere carrier for hire. Again, we speak of a porter as the attendant at, or the custodian of, the entrance gate of a mansion or public building. In the one case the porter is a very humble

---

[1] Plutarch, *Symp.*, Bk. ii, Quest, 5, §2.

[2] See Smith's *Dict. Of Greek and Roman Antiq.* s.vv."Athletae," and "Olympic Games;" Gardner's *New Chapters in Greek History*, pp. 297-302.

personage, in the other case he is a person of responsibility and importance. How it came about that the same term is applied to both these personages is worth considering, in view of its bearing on the importance of the door and the gate.

It is said to have been a custom of the ancient Etruscans and Romans, and perhaps of older peoples, in laying out the foundations of a city, to mark first the compass of the whole city with a plow. When they came to those places where they were to have the gates of the city, they took up the plow and carried it across the gateway, "transported" the plow at that space. It is said that from this custom the Latin word *porta* came to apply to "a gate," "*a portando aratrum*," "from carrying the plow," —*porta*, in Latin, meaning "to carry." Whether or not the traditional custom referred to had a historical basis, it will be seen that the mere fact of the tradition will account for the twofold use, in languages derived from the Latin, of the word "porter" as a carrier, and again as a door-keeper, or a gate watcher, or a guardian of the threshold. Apart from the question of the origin of the terms, we find that the porter or carrier is one who goes through the gate as the place of entrance or exit in his carryings; or, again, the porter or guardian of the gate is one who watches the place of carryings, and of outgoing and incoming.

Among the stories told of the founding of Rome by Romulus, it is said that at the threshold of this enterprise the people kindled fires before their tents, and then leaped through or over the flames.[1] In connection with this

---

[1] A primitive wedding ceremony. See pp. 39-42, 142f., 212, supra.

ceremony sacrifices were offered, and offerings of the first-fruits of forest and field were made to the gods.[1] A heifer and a bull were yoked to the plow, as in symbol of marriage, and afterwards were offered in sacrifice, thus supplying the symbolic blood on the threshold of the new city. [2] Plutarch, it is true, thinks that, in consequence of this custom of laying out a city, the walls of a city, *except the gates,* were counted sacred; but in this, as in other matters relating to the threshold,[3] it is evident that Plutarch was not sure to be correct as to the meaning of archaic customs.

There seems to be force in the suggestion that the two Latin words, *porta* and *porta,* like the Greek *poros,* were derived from the common Aryan root *par* or *por,* "to go," "to bring over," "to pass through."[4] However this may be, we have the common English use of the term "port" in words meaning a door or entrance, and again a carrying or a place of carriage, as "export," "import," "transport," "portico," "porthole," "portfolio," etc.

An illustration of the twofold use of the word is found in the word "a portage" or "a carry" as the designation of "a break in a chain of water communication over which goods, boats, etc., have to be carried, as from one lake or river to another." It is not merely that this is a place where a canoe, or other luggage, must be carried, but it is the definite

---

[1] See, again, pp. 16f., 46f., supra.

[2] See *Plutarch's Lives,*"Romulus;" also references to Strabo, and Dionysius of Halicarnassus, in Hooke's *Roman History,* I., 42.

[3] See references at pp. 39, 263, supra.

[4] See Skeat's *Etymological Dictionary and the Century Dictionary,* s.v.

"carry" or "portage," the bridge, or isthmus, or door, or threshold,[1] by which they enter another region. This is the common American use of the term in pioneer life.[2]

PASSING OVER INTO A COVENANT

As these pages are going to press, Dr. Sailer calls my attention to the phrase לעבר בברית *la'abhor bibereeth,* to enter, or pass over, into a covenant. This phrase, as Dr. Driver[3] points out, is found only in one place, at Deuteronomy 29:12. "That thou shouldest enter [or pass] into the covenant of the Lord thy God, and into his oath, which the Lord thy God maketh with thee this day."

It is evident that here is the idea of passing over a line or boundary, or threshold limit, into another region, or state or condition. Until that threshold is crossed, the person is outside of the covenant with its privileges and benefits; but when it is crossed, or passed, the person is a partaker of all that is within.

This word *'abhar* corresponds with, while it differs from, the word *pasakh*. The two words have, indeed, been counted by some lexicographers as practically equivalents. Thus Furst[4] gives *'pasakh = 'abhar.'* In the covenant

---

[1] See p. 180f., supra.

[2] See "portage" in *the Century Dictionary*, with examples of usage.

[3] Driver's *Deuteronomy,* p. 323.

[4] *Heb. Chald. Lex.,* s.v.

which Jehovah makes with Abraham, for himself and his posterity (Gen.15:1-21), when the heifer and the she goat and the ram had been slaughtered and divided, and the pieces laid over against each other as two walls, or sides of a door, with the blood probably poured out on the earth as a threshold between, "a smoking furnace and a flaming torch,"—representing the divine presence—"passed," or covenant-crossed, the blood on the threshold "between these pieces," between these fleshly walls or door-posts of the sacrifice.[1]

In Jeremiah 34:18, the word appears in its twofold signification, in conjunction with a similar double use of the word *karath* ("to cut"). Jehovah says, "I will give the men that have transgressed [*'abhar*, crossed or passed] my covenant . . . which they made [cut] before me when they cut the calf in twain and passed [over its blood] between the parts thereof." Again, in Amos 7:8, Jehovah says of his reprobate people, "I will not again pass by [*'abhar*] them [covenant-cross them] any more."

There seems to be a trace of this cross-over, or pass-over, covenant idea in the references to the passing through the fire in the worship of false gods, as at 2 Kings 16:3, where King Ahaz is said to have "walked in the way of the kings of Israel, yea, and made his son to pass through [*'abhar*] the fire, according to the abominations of the heathen."[2] It is evident that this passing through the fire in

---

[1] See p. 187f., supra.

[2] See, also, 2 Kings 21:6; 23:10; 2 Chron. 33:6; Ezek. 16:21; 20:26, 31; 23:37.

APPENDIX

honor of a false god was not the being thrown into the fire
as a burnt offering; for such sacrifices are referred to by
themselves, as a Deuteronomy 12:31, where it is said of the
people of Jehovah that "even their sons and their daughters
do they burn [*saraph*] in the fire to their gods."[1] In the same
chapter of 2 Kings (17:17,31) the two phases of causing
children to "pass through" the fire, and of "burning"
children in the fire, are separately referred to, in illustration
of the fact that they are not one and the same thing.

It has already been shown[2] that jumping across, or
being lifted over, a fire, at the threshold, is an ancient mode
of covenanting, still surviving in many marriage or other
customs; and that the blood of both human and substitute
sacrifices has often been poured out at the same primitive
altar.

Under the figure of a marriage covenant Jehovah
speaks, in Ezekiel 16:8, of entering into a covenant, when
he takes the virgin Israel as his bride: "Yea, I sware unto
thee, and entered into a covenant with thee, saith the Lord
God, and thou becamest mine." Here the more common
word *bo* is used for the idea of entering; but its connection
with the covenant of marriage would seem to connect it, like
the other words, *pasach* and *'abhar*, with the thought of
crossing over the threshold or barrier into a new state.

[1] See, also, Jer. 7:31; 19:5.

[2] See pp. 39-42, 142f., 212, supra.

ENGLAND'S CORONATION STONE.

A notable survival of the primitive reverence for the one foundation, or the original threshold, as the earliest place of sacrifice and covenanting,[1] is shown in the famous "Coronation Stone" in Westminster Abbey. This stone is under the chair in which all the sovereigns of England from Edward I. to Victoria have been crowned. It was brought by Edward I. to England from Scone, the coronation seat of the kings of Scotland. The legend attached to it was that it was the stone pillar on which Jacob rested at Bethel,—the House of God where Abraham worshiped, and where Jacob covenanted with God for all of his generations.[2]

"In it, or upon it, the Kings of Scotland were placed by the Earls of Fife. From it Scone became the *'sedis principalis'* of Scotland, and the kingdom of Scotland the kingdom of Scone." Since the days of Edward I., it has never been removed from Westminster Abbey, except when Cromwell was installed as Lord Protector in Westminster Hall, on which occasion it was brought out in order that he might be placed on it.

As in ancient Babylonia, in Egypt, in Syria, in India, in China, in Arabia, in Greece, in Scandinavia, the one primitive foundation was deemed the only foundation on

---

[1] See pp. 153-164, supra.

[2] See Dean Stanley's *Historical Memorials of Westminster Abbey*, first edition, pp. 59-67; also, Appendices, pp. 492-502.

which to build securely with divine approval, so in the very center of the highest modern civilization the reputed foundation stone of the kingdom of the "Father of the Faithful" is deemed the only secure coronation, or installation, seat of King, Queen, or Lord Protector. Is it not reasonable to suppose that this feeling has a basis in primitive religious convictions and customs?

Dean Stanley, referring to this Coronation Stone as "probably the chief object of attraction to the innumerable visitors to the Abbey," says of it: "It is the one primeval monument which binds together the whole Empire. The iron rings, the battered surface, the crack which has all but rent its solid mass asunder, bear witness to its long migrations. It is thus embedded in the heart of the English monarchy—an element of poetic, patriarchal, heathen times, which, like Araunah's rocky threshing floor in the midst of the Temple of Solomon, carries back our thoughts to races and customs now almost extinct; a link which unites the Throne of England to the traditions of Tara and Iona, and connects the charm of our complex civilization with the forces of our mother earth,—the stocks and stones of savage nature."[1]

---

[1] See Dean Stanley's *Historical Memorials of Westminster Abbey*, first edition, pp. 64-66.

SUPPLEMENT.

SUPPLEMENT.

Before their publishing, the proof-sheets of this volume were submitted to a number of prominent scholars in Europe and America, for their examination and comment, in order to ascertain if the main thought of the work seemed justified by the facts known to them in their several special fields of knowledge and study. Some of the opinions and suggestions of these scholars as given herewith will have deservedly, in the eyes of many readers, a weight and value beyond anything that could be said by the author of this work.

FROM THE REV. DR. MARCUS JASTROW.

As a Jewish clergyman, and as a conservative Bible scholar, the Rev. Dr. Jastrow is honored on both sides of the Atlantic for his special attainments in Talmudic and Rabbinical lore. His great work, "A *Dictionary of the Targumim, the Talmud Babli and Yerushalmi, and the Midrashic Literature*," is a monument of his learning and ability in these fields. He writes:

"I have read your interesting work, 'The Threshold Covenant,' with great attention, and derived from it more information than I can possibly thank you for.

"As I am unable to form an independent opinion on the bearing of your evidences on the thesis of your work, I can refer only to those parts of it which treat of Jewish customs and ideas, and, here, I feel it a privilege to be permitted to say that I admire your ingenious conception of the passover covenant in Egypt. Especially interesting, and undoubtedly correct, is your interpretation of Exodus 12:23, according to which the Lord passes over the threshold in order to visit the Israelitish house, and will not allow the destroyer to enter.

"It may not be out of place here to direct your attention to a passage in Talmud Yerushalmi, Aboda Zaaara III,42d, where it is said about the Philistines: 'They revered the threshold (*miftan*) more

245

than the Dagon,' to which is added, 'All other nations made (worshiped) only one *miftan*, but the Israelites made many *miftanoth*,' which explains the verse, 'And I will visit punishment on him who leaps, and on the *miftan*' (Zeph.1:9). You will observe that the Talmud quotes the verse different from the Massoretic text, which reads, 'on every one who leaps over the *miftan.'* I am unable to decide whether the deviation from the Massoretic text is owing to a different text before the Talmudic authority under consideration, or merely to a slip of memory, such as often occurs with those who quote from memory.

"In Talmud Babli, referring to the Philistines in relation to the Dagon, it is said: 'They let alone the Dagon and worshiped the *miftan*, for they said, His prince (genius) has abandoned the Dagon and has come to sit on the *miftan*.' All of which proves that there lingered yet in the memory of the Talmudists the traditional recollection of *miftan* worship."

FROM PROFESSOR DR. HERMAN V. HILPRECHT.

Oldest among civilizations of which we have any sure record is that of Babylonia. Among the foremost scholars in that realm is Dr. Hilprecht, formerly of the University of Erlangen, and now Professor of Assyriology in the University of Pennsylvania. His prominence is recognized in Europe as fully as in America. His labors, in the field and in the study, in connection with the successful Babylonian Expedition of the University of Pennsylvania, and his monumental work, still in course of publication, on the Cuneiform Texts brought to light by that expedition, have added to his reputation on both sides of the ocean, and confirmed his high standing among the best scholars of the world in his special department of knowledge.

It was while on his way to Constantinople, to examine the latest "finds" in Babylonia brought to the Imperial Museum there, with which museum Professor Hilprecht has an official connection, that he examined the proof-sheets of "The Threshold Covenant." Of the work in its entirety he writes in generous appreciation as follows:

246

"Your latest book, 'The Threshold Covenant," accompanied me on my trip to Constantinople. Before we had crossed the Atlantic I had studied it three times from beginning to end. I take the first opportunity, at Southhampton, to send you these lines, in order to express to you my full appreciation of what you have offered to the scientific world in your magnificent work.

"If in your former book, 'The Blood Covenant,' you made (as was suggested by an eminent German theologian) the first successful attempt to write a theology of the blood, you have given us in your most recent work a thorough investigation on the significance and history of the primitive altar upon which blood was shed by men entering into a covenant with God or their fellow-men. Surely your two books 'The Blood Covenant,' and 'The Threshold Covenant' belong together, and should therefore be studied together. One supplements the other, and the former furnishes the key to a full understanding of the facts presented in the latter; and so again on the other side.

It must have cost you decenniums to gather all the materials which you lay before the reader in such a systematic form. All the nations of the world, civilized and uncivilized, ancient and modern, seem to have contributed their share to your stately structure, which has my full admiration. Viewed in this light alone, your book will always prove a regular storehouse, of knowledge for students of primitive rites and religions, and of various other kindred subjects.

"It is, of course, impossible for any specialist in one certain line to fully estimate the hundreds of new features presented in your recent work. It would be bold on my part, at least, to express an opinion on questions with which I am not entirely familiar. As, however, you treat facts which bear closely upon my special line of investigation,—the oldest history, languages, and civilization of the Euphrates valley, and of their rites in general ,—I can heartily assure you that, according to my examination, you have proved your main points beyond question.

"It is first of all sure that you are the first who fully recognized, and in fact rediscovered, the world-wide importance and fundamental significance of the threshold in all ancient religions. You have reeestablished an ancient rite which was practically entirely forgotten by modern scholars. By restoring the threshold to its proper place in primitive religions, you have rendered a great service to comparative religion, archeology, and even philology. Many a statement by ancient writers was obscure to us, many a word puzzling as to its original etymology and significance, and not a few facts brought to light by recent excavations remained incoherent and mysterious, because we had lost sight of the significance of the threshold, which, very appropriately, you style the first altar of the human race.

"In reading your book I could not help wondering that all these combinations which appear quite clear and plausible now were not made a long while ago by other investigators. The earliest inscribed monuments of ancient Babylonia, dating from the fifth millennium before Christ, are door-sockets which bear ample witness to the correctness of your theory. Professor Hommel's recent ingenious analysis of the Assyrian word for "to pray," which was a result of his study of your 'Threshold Covenant,' is one of the strongest evidences in favor of your arguments. Our own recent excavations of the lowest strata of the temple of Bel in Nippur, which takes us back to 7000 B.C., testify in the same direction.

"Of the greatest importance for the study of the Old Testament religion is your doubtless correct explanation of the Passover. It is entirely in harmony with ancient customs, with philology, and with common sense. According to the old interpretation this rite hangs, so to speak, in the air, without any connection, and yet we know from many other instances that Old Testament rites of the Hebrews stand in the closest possible connection with those practiced by surrounding nations. In the light of your investigations I regard it as an established fact, and as one of the chief results of your labors, that Jehovah in entering into covenant with his 'bride Israel' did not invent a new rite, but took one with which his chosen people were already familiar, and gave to it a new and deeper significance in its new use and relations.

"Your final chapter, 'Outgrowths and Perversions of this Rite,' is likewise full of thought and new suggestions. One cannot help wishing you might have gone beyond the scope of your book and expressed yourself more in detail as to the precise connection in which tree and phallus worship stand to the threshold in each of the principal ancient religions, and what role the snake played in the further development or determination of the primitive rite so excellently discussed by you. There is no doubt in my mind that all these different rites, however independent of each other they may appear in later times, are but different outgrowths of the same original root and later perversions of original uplifting thought,—search for unity between men and God. But as you yourself have given only brief indications of this, I wisely abstain from entering into details.

"Permit me to congratulate you upon the completion of a work which, in the nature of things, must attract the general attention of scholars. Whatever may be the interpretation of certain details contained in your book, the one fact remains sure: it will always be your great merit to have penetrated into the long-forgotten secrets of one of the most ancient rites of humanity, and, by pointing out its great importance for and its connection with other rites, to have constructed a solid basis for further investigations, and to have put loose facts together, and given them a well-defined place in a regular system."

It is undoubtedly true that the fresh material from the excavations at Nippur will furnish additional illustrations of the main thesis of this work. Dr. Hilprecht will be sure to note these.

FROM PROFESSOR DR. FRITZ HOMMEL.

As an Arabist as well as an Assyriologist, and as a bright thinker and learned scholar, in various departments of knowledge, Dr. Fritz Hommel, Professor of Semitic Languages in the University of Munich, has a deservedly high standing. His great illustrated "*History of Babylonia and Assyria*" is a marvelous treasure-house of information concerning the history of the earlier civilizations of the East; and his later studies in connection with the researches of Dr. Edward Glaser in South Arabia have poured a flood of light on the influence of ancient Arabia in the Oriental world. In the realm of Semitic philology Dr. Hommel is acute minded, and peculiarly alert and suggestive.

Having read the earlier pages of "The Threshold Covenant," Professor Hommel wrote briefly of his interest in the main thought of the work, and promised further comments when he has completed its examination. The necessity of putting these pages to press forbids the waiting for his valued conclusions. His first comments are:

"I am now reading with great interest the proof-sheets of your new book, which you were kind enough to send me. Although at this moment overburdened with other work, I have already got as far as page 70, and hope in the course of a fortnight to be able to send you my judgment.

"To page 60 I wish now to note that already in the time of Hammurabi disputes were settled at the gate, and, indeed, of the gate of the temple. See Strassmaier's Warka Tablets, 30 (B.57) in Meissner's *Beitraze Zum Altbabylonishchen Privatraecht*, p.42f.

"An interesting discovery, of which perhaps you still may make use, I made yesterday. It is that the Babylonian SUPPU ('to pray,' 'to entreat') is originally merely the verb formed from the noun SIPPU, 'a threshold.' The first sense, indeed, of SUPPU is 'to sacrifice,' because that was done at the threshold. To find a parallel for this transference from the meaning 'to offer' to the meaning 'to pray, compare the Arabic '*atara*, to sacrifice,' with the Hebrew '*atar*, to pray.' To this discovery I, of course, came through your deductions with regard to the importance of the threshold."

FROM PROFESSOR DR. A. H. SAYCE.

No Oriental scholar and archeologist is more widely known in Europe and America, and beyond, or is surer of a hearing on any subject of which he writes, from both those who agree and those who differ with him, than Professor Sayce of Oxford University. The numerous published works of Professor Sayce have made him extensively known among scholars, and popularly. Prominent among these are the Hibbert Lectures on "The Religion of the Ancient Babylonians," "The Ancient Empires of the East," "Fresh Light from Ancient Monuments," "The Life and Times of Isaiah," "the Hittites," "Patriarchal Palestine," and "The Egypt of the Hebrews." He now writes from Luxor, in Egypt, while passing the winter, as usual, on the Nile, in his dahabiyeh Istar:

"A thousand thanks for the advance sheets of 'The Threshold Covenant.' Like all your work, it is brimful of accurate knowledge and new points of view, and is written so charmingly that a child could understand and follow you. I need not say I have been devouring the pages and admiring their wealth of references. While I read, you carried me along with you, and, if you had asked my opinion as I went on, I should have said that you had made out your case step by step. But now that I come to look back upon the work as a whole, the skeptical side of my nature comes uppermost, and I have an uneasy feeling that the proof is too complete. That you have made out your case to a large extent is clear, but whether allowance ought not to be made for other elements is not so clear to me. Human nature is complex, and we still know so little about the early history of civilized man! And between civilized and uncivilized man the gulf seems to have always been as great as it is today."

FROM PROFESSOR DR. W. MAX MULLER.

As an Egyptologist, Professor Muller is recognized for his scholarship and learning on both sides of the Atlantic. A favorite pupil of Georg Ebers, he continued his studies at the University of Berlin under Adolf Erman, and soon made a mark for himself. His *Asien und Europe Nach Altagypt Denkmaller,*—"Asia and Europe from the Egyptian Monuments,"—at once gave him high standing in that field. Expressing his regret that he was not able to give more time to the examination of "The Threshold Covenant" in its proof-sheets, he says:

"You did not hear from me earlier because my too close occupation prevented my studying your book as thoroughly as I wished, and contributing, as I hoped to, something on the threshold question. Even now I have to write hastily.

"I have found your book most interesting and suggestive, so that I heartily recommend its publication. I hope to be able to read it more carefully, and to give a more detailed criticism, after a while.

"A few remarks:

"Page 103.—*per-ao* (Pharaoh)—gate, door. Not to be proved. Strangely, the root *pire* means 'to go out.' Originally *pr* may have been 'door,' but not in historic times.

"Page 161.—(Calling the region of Sinai, the 'land of God'.) A mistake! The 'land of God' is only the land on the Red Sea. No such records known of Mt. Sinai.

"Page 180, line 5.—(A memorial stone spoken of as marking the boundary line.) How do you know it was a boundary stone?

"There is rich material of better and earlier passages on boundary stones than that given on page 180.

"*El gisr* means 'bridge.' The dictionaries do not give 'threshold.'

"Page 184.—Sinai, an 'Egyptian boundary line'? Still less did the 'holy mountain' (p.185) ever mark the southern frontier. The threshold sacrifices are evidently a mistake. But I do not have at hand Brugsch's book—a very fanciful and unreliable book.

"I hope that as soon as a very pressing work has been finished, I shall be able to revise all your passages bearing on Egypt. But even if I should find some more of these minor faults, they would not change the good general impression of the book."

It will be seen that none of the points questioned by Professor Muller are vital to the main thesis of the book, or essential to its illustration of the prevalence of the threshold.

INDEX.

SCRIPTURAL INDEX.

SCRIPTURAL INDEX.

SCRIPTURAL INDEX.

A BLOOD COVENANT
IS THE MOST
SOLEMN, BINDING AGREEMENT POSSIBLE
BETWEEN TWO PARTIES.

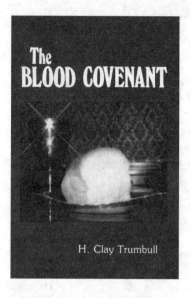

Perhaps one of the least understood, and yet most important and relevant factors necessary for an appreciation of the series of covenants and covenant relationships that our God has chosen to employ in His dealings with man, is the concept of the BLOOD COVENANT!

In this volume which has been "sold out," and "unavailable" for generations, lies truth which has blessed and will continue to bless every pastor, teacher, every serious Christian desiring to "go on with God."

Andrew Murray stated it beautifully years ago, when he said that if we were to but grasp the full knowledge of what God desires to do for us and understood the nature of His promises, it would "make the Covenant the very gate of heaven! May the Holy Spirit give us some vision of its glory."

$10.95 + 2.00 postage and handling

The
Acts
of
Pilate

ANCIENT RECORDS RECORDED BY
CONTEMPORARIES OF JESUS CHRIST
REGARDING THE FACTS CONCERNING
HIS BIRTH, DEATH, RESURRECTION

◆

TRANSLATED FROM THE ORIGINAL LANGUAGES
BY DRS. MCINTOSH and TWYMAN

◆

EDITED BY REV. W.D. MAHAN

This book was a favorite of the late Kathryn Kuhlman who often read from it on her radio show.

Early Church Writers such as Justin refer to the existence of these records, and Tertullian specifically mentions the report made by Pilate to the Emperor of Rome, Tiberius Caesar.

Chapters Include:
+ *How These Records Were Discovered,*
+ *A Short Sketch of the Talmuds,*
+ *Constantine's Letter in Regard to Having Fifty Copies of the Scriptures Written and Bound,*
+ *Jonathan's Interview with the Bethlehem Shepherds Letter of Melker, Priest of the Synagogue at Bethlehem,*
+ *Gamaliel's Interview with Joseph and Mary and Others Concerning Jesus,*
+ *Report of Caiaphas to the Sanhedrim Concerning the Resurrection of Jesus,*
+ *Valleus's Notes — "Acta Pilati," or Pilate's Report to Caesar of the Arrest, Trial, and Crucifixion of Jesus,*
+ *Herod Antipater's Defense Before the Roman Senate in Regard to His Conduct At Bethlehem,*
+ *Herod Antipas's Defense Before the Roman Senate in Regard to the Execution of John the Baptist,*
+ *The Hillel Letters Regarding God's Providence to the Jews, by Hillel the Third*

THE ACTS OF PILATE $9.95, plus $2.00 Shipping

IMPACT CHRISTIAN BOOKS, INC.
332 Leffingwell Ave., Suite 101, Kirkwood, MO 63122

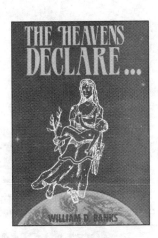

Impact Christian Books

332 Leffingwell Ave., Suite 101
Kirkwood, MO 63122